PULLED WORK
ON CANVAS AND LINEN

BOOKS BY ROSEMARY DRYSDALE

The Art of Blackwork Embroidery

Pulled Work on Canvas and Linen

To KENT and SHONA
for all their patience

CONTENTS

ACKNOWLEDGMENTS

I would like to extend my thanks to Joan Toggitt for her constant encouragement; Rene Farber, Althea Gardner, Sharon Halper, and Nancy Stolavsky for stitching many of the samples in the book; to my students and friends who gave me permission to publish their work; and to Kent Carroll for the photography.

PULLED WORK
ON CANVAS AND LINEN

INTRODUCTION

CANVAS WORK has become one of the most popular forms of embroidery in America. Both the standard of work and the variety of stitches have greatly improved since the painted needlepoint canvas days.

Now that more people are familiar with counting threads and following graphs, new techniques to express creative talent are needed. The beautiful lacy patterns of pulled work are a natural next step for canvas work. In the past, pulled stitches were usually worked in white on fine, even-weave linen. Although extremely beautiful and delicate, this exacting work may not be suitable for the canvas worker of today. Anyone wishing to make such delicate pieces, however, can of course work all the stitches in this book on even-weave linen or very fine canvas instead of the medium canvas suggested.

Canvas threads are clear and easy to count, and counting threads is the basis for pulled work. Therefore, pulled work on canvas is the simplest way to introduce pulled work to the needleworker.

What Is Pulled Work?

Pulled work (known as drawn fabric in Britain), as the name implies, is the pulling tightly of stitches so that the ground material, in this case the canvas, comes together to form holes. By pulling various stitches tightly, the holes form patterns often referred to as *fillings*.

Pull Tight

As you make each stitch you must pull the yarn in the needle very tightly. This may be a little difficult to master at first, as most of us have been taught for years *not* to pull too tightly.

Although the stitches must be pulled tightly, constant tension and rhythm are essential to produce an even, beautiful effect. In pulled work, the most difficult skill to master is pulling your stitches tight enough while, at the same time, keeping an even tension. As in any other craft, the more you practice the easier it becomes.

History

I will not attempt to give you a detailed account of the development of pulled work, as my main concern is the teaching of the stitches and their application to designs. However, histories are fascinating and I am sure many readers will enjoy delving into old books and museum textile collections to see what they can discover about this art.

It is interesting to speculate about the origin of pulled work. The most obvious explanation is that the art was simply a result of some needleworkers pulling their stitches too tightly, inadvertently producing holes. These holes, as we know, were pleasing to the eye and resembled lace.

In the past almost all pulled work was done in monochrome on fine, even-weave linen and used for household articles and clothing. It became extremely popular during the eighteenth century, especially in Denmark and Britain, and was a means of duplicating the fine laces of the period which were time-consuming to make and expensive to buy. Pulled work of this nature required tremendous skill and patience, and the fine examples we see in museums today lead us to believe that the pieces were worked by professional embroiderers.

During the eighteenth century pulled work was seldom used by itself. Rather, it was integrated with other embroidery techniques on the same article to provide a delicate, lacy effect.

Although we have identified samples of pulled work dating as far back as the fourteenth century, the art attained its highest standards only during the eighteenth century. Fine examples can be found on old embroideries from Greece and Russia. The designs are more peasantlike than the pieces from Western Europe, but they have a charm and simplicity we can still admire. The Greek and Near Eastern work is unique in that yarn was used in one or more colors that contrasted with the fabric, such as black and red stitching on white linen. In Britain matching yarn and fabric were the norm, usually white yarn on white linen.

Some of the finest examples of counted-thread work as an embroidery technique have come from the Scandinavians. They have long used pulled work stitches in their famous geometric as well as realistic designs, and the clean, even work and symmetry of their patterns are magnificent. Many design books showing lovely examples of Scandinavian pulled work are available (see the reading list at the back of the book).

Early Americans were less involved in pulled work than needleworkers in some European countries. The exception was the American settlers of Scandinavian descent who handed down the tradition of counted-thread work from generation to generation. Early American samplers feature some fine examples of pulled stitches.

MATERIALS
AND TECHNIQUES

FOR PULLED WORK the fabric must have an even weave—that is, the same number of weft threads as warp threads. Needlepoint canvas is ideal. This canvas comes in two kinds: mono (single threads) and Penelope (double threads). Use only mono canvas and never use a canvas with an interlocked weave.

Canvas is made in both cotton and linen. The linen is more suitable for pulled work, but as it is very expensive I would suggest that a beginner start with a good-quality cotton.

Canvas is sold by number—that is, the number of woven threads to the inch. For example, a number 14 canvas means that fourteen warp threads and fourteen weft threads are woven to the square inch. A number 22 canvas has twenty-two warp threads and twenty-two weft threads per square inch and therefore is a finer canvas, as the threads are closer together.

A number 14 canvas is suitable for most pulled work, but I am sure that as your standards rise and your ability improves you will find yourself working finer pulled work on number 18 and number 20 canvas.

Buy the best-quality canvas you can find and check for pieces with knotted repairs: refuse them. Also avoid heavily sized flimsy canvas.

I use a French or German canvas and find it can be washed successfully in cold water, stretched again into a square shape, and even ironed flat. Sometimes I wash the canvas before I begin my pulled work, as washing makes the canvas softer and this makes it easier to pull the stitches into patterns.

Most canvas is woven only in white. If you like other colors, dye your canvas with a commercial dye, preferably a cold-water dye (Dylon), following the instructions on the packet. Be sure to stretch your canvas square again while it is drying. It is also advisable to machine or hand stitch a 1/4-inch single turning all around the canvas before washing or dyeing, to prevent unraveling.

Frames

Embroidery frames are sold in various lengths. They hold the canvas taut and keep the threads straight and easier to count. Do not use a circular hoop, which distorts the canvas weave.

Needles

Needles without points (tapestry needles) should be used, because a point will split the canvas threads. Tapestry needles are sold by number; the higher the number, the finer the needle. A number 22 is a comfortable size to work with. The eye of the needle must be large enough to take the yarn without rubbing so as to avoid fraying. The needle should not be so thick as to push the canvas threads out of place.

Yarns

The yarn used in pulled work must be very strong and preferably twisted. Linen yarns are the best but they are difficult to obtain. The yarns listed below are also suitable:

Fawcett linen yarn, available in many colors and weights

Buttonhole twist

Crochet yarns—for example, Knit-Cro-Sheen, D.M.C.

Cordonnet

D.M.C. coton à broder

D.M.C. pearl cotton, available in many weights

Fine string

Silk thread

Stranded embroidery floss and tapestry wool may also be used, but because of the tension required in pulled work they tend to fray and will sometimes break.

The weight of yarn chosen should correspond to the weight of the fabric threads to be stitched, the idea being that the working yarn should, in effect, become part of the fabric. The designs are made by the holes the stitches create and not by the stitches themselves.

Always remember that the working yarn should not untwist. To avoid untwisting, use strands no longer than 18 inches.

Notes on Using Even-Weave Linen

You may want to use some of your pulled work pieces for table linens and clothing. Canvas is not suitable for this purpose; therefore, I suggest you use an even-weave linen. You work the stitches in exactly the same manner as on canvas, but because the linen is not as stiff as the canvas you need not pull as tightly. At first, working on linen will be a strange experience, as the linen will feel soft and flimsy compared to canvas. Work an even-weave linen sampler until you feel at ease with the fabric before you begin any finished piece. Once you have discovered even-weave linens you may well become addicted to them.

Always turn a single hem around the edges of the linen before stitching. A good guide for deciding the weight of the yarn to use is to match the yarn to one of the threads of the linen—they should be the same thickness. Since you do not need to pull so tightly on linen, embroidery floss is ideal to work with.

Linen, like canvas, is sold by the number. I suggest nineteen threads to the inch for a beginner. One of the advantages to linen is that, unlike canvas, it is made in beautiful colors.

A list of suppliers is given at the back of the book.

See the photograph of the linen place mat and napkin opposite.

Helpful Hints for Working Pulled Work on Canvas and Linen

1. Always secure the edges of the canvas with masking tape before starting to stitch. Oversew or machine stitch the edges of the linen.

2. Whenever possible, use a frame.

3. Have a sharp pair of pointed scissors on hand for picking out mistakes.

4. Always have a sampler accompanying each piece of work for practicing stitches and effects.

Linen place mat and napkin.

5. Avoid using a variety of stitches on one piece of work. Simplicity is best.

6. Use monochrome effects—for example, light blue on blue. Pulled work is most effective when the stitches blend into the fabric, producing the effect of being part of the woven piece. The holes make the patterns. If you do use color, work with a single color on a contrasting background, such as red on white.

7. Avoid picking out threads, because this causes the fabric to go out of shape. If you must do so, stroke the fabric threads back into place with your needle.

8. Always have clean hands when working and a basket or cloth to hold the work when not in use.

9. Understand the stitch diagrams very well before attempting a finished piece. Remember, on the instruction graphs each line represents a thread of the fabric and each square a space between the threads.

10. Practice and know each stitch before attempting a large piece of work.

11. Beginning and ending a thread:

The method of beginning and ending a thread depends on the design and the stitch being worked.

When the design has been outlined, simply begin and end by weaving the thread through the worked outline stitches, taking a couple of tiny backstitches to secure it.

When the design is not being outlined, as in the case of many geometric patterns, begin with a few tiny running stitches and a backstitch worked on the line, which will then be covered by the stitches to be made. Or begin with a "waste knot." This is a knot placed on the front of the work about 3 inches from where the stitching is to begin. After working a few stitches, cut off the knot, rethread the tail into the needle, and weave it through the back of the stitches to ensure that it is securely attached.

To end a thread, weave it through the backs of the previously worked stitches. Be sure, however, to get the pull of the very last stitch slanting in the correct direction before you begin to end off the thread. Also be very careful, when beginning and ending a thread, never to work the thread across the holes of the fillings; it will show on the front of your work and ruin the lacy appearance.

It sometimes happens that a thread must be joined in the middle of a row of stitches. In such a case weave the old thread into the fabric as invisibly as possible in the forward direction. Then weave the new thread into the backs of the previously worked stitches. This ensures a continuous line where the join is, thus avoiding making the joined stitches slope in the wrong direction.

12. Working from row to row:

Many stitches are worked in one direction only. At the end of each row fasten off the thread and begin another row. Remember always to work in the same direction.

Some stitches can be worked backward and forward; you turn the work as you go. However, you must take special care to ensure that the correct "pull" is made on the last stitch before turning the work to start the next row. To ensure this, I take my thread onto the wrong side after the last stitch has been worked and slip it behind the back of the stitch in the direction of my next row. This secures the pull of my last stitch. Practice makes working from row to row much easier than lengthy directions and diagrams.

13. Stretching finished pieces:

When all the stitchery is completed, your work will be a little out of shape, so it must be stretched.

To do this, wet the piece with cold water, then tack it, right side up, on a board over blotting paper or a terry towel. Be sure to use rust-proof push pins. Place the pins about ½ inch apart, keeping the piece of fabric square.

Allow the piece to dry; then, if necessary, carefully press it on a soft pad wrong side down, using a damp cloth and a hot iron.

14. When making a geometric design, always baste the center of the fabric with a colored thread before starting. This will ensure a well-balanced piece.

The Use of the Sampler

Some people do not understand the use of a sampler. A sampler is not a finished piece of work to be framed or made into a pillow. It is similar to an artist's sketchbook and is a place on which to experiment and practice.

Whenever a new piece of work is started, it should be accompanied by a sampler of exactly the same fabric and yarns. The sampler is the place to discover how to work with the materials chosen for the finished piece.

On the sampler practice the stitches you intend to use, and experiment with them until you are satisfied. Experiment by using different yarns and changing the scale of the stitches.

When you are satisfied with your choice of stitches, begin your finished piece and keep your sampler at hand as a "reference book."

YOUR PULLED WORK SAMPLER

It is important that you have a sampler on which to practice the pulled stitches in this book. To make a sampler all you need are the following:

1. A 15-inch-square piece of mono canvas, number 14 (edges taped with masking tape), or a 15-inch-square piece of even-weave linen, nineteen threads per inch (edges stitched to prevent fraying)
2. A number 22 tapestry needle
3. White or ecru D.M.C. pearl cotton number 5

Now refer to page 21 and practice the satin stitch, first working it without pulling and then pulling very tightly and evenly. At first your stitches may be irregular if you are not pulling with an even tension. Once your stitches are even, go on to the satin stitch fillings on pages 54–60.

Make a new sampler for other fillings. Also try working with various yarns so that you see their effects when pulled. You may even alter the size of your stitch by counting over six threads instead of four, or by changing to a finer canvas. Experiment and make as many samplers as possible. We never know enough to give up making samplers.

THE STITCHES

In the following pages you will learn how to work many stitches. The diagrams show the method of working each stitch; for the sake of clarity, the pull on the stitch is not shown. Threads on the front of the work are shown as solid lines on the diagrams, and the broken lines indicate the threads on the back of the work.

Line Stitches Worked Horizontally and Vertically

Line stitches are used as frames and borders for designs and as connections between shapes. When worked together in rows they form *fillings,* and when worked in conjunction with other stitches they form *composite fillings.*

SATIN STITCH

This is sometimes called whipped stitch and can be worked without pulling or be "pulled" to various degrees to produce different effects. Satin stitch is a simple stitch to work and has many uses. It can

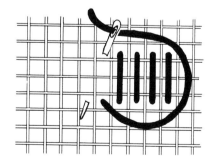

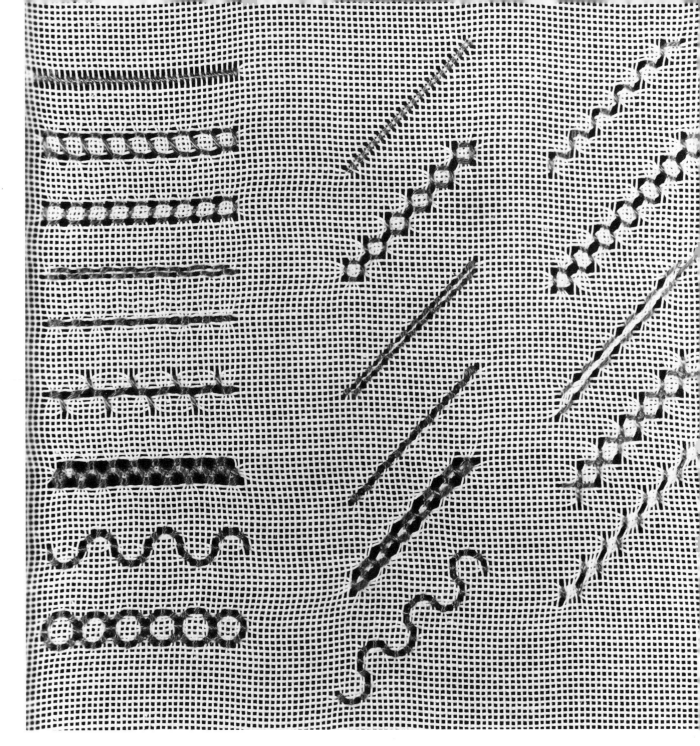

Line stitches worked horizontally and diagonally.

Horizontal stitches (LEFT FROM TOP TO BOTTOM): satin stitch, flat square stitch, raised square stitch, chained border stitch, backstitch, backstitch variation, three-sided stitch, waved backstitch, ringed backstitch.

Diagonal stitches (CENTER): diagonal satin stitch, diagonal raised square stitch, diagonal chained border stitch, diagonal backstitch, diagonal three-sided stitch, diagonal waved backstitch.

Diagonal stitches (RIGHT): single faggot stitch, double faggot stitch, reversed faggot stitch, Greek cross stitch, Indian drawn ground.

be worked from right to left, or horizontally or vertically. The most important factor is to keep the stitches on the right side straight and those on the wrong side slanted.

When worked in a single line the working yarn is pulled upward at right angles to the fabric, whereas when two rows are worked, work the first row with the pull away from you and the second row with the pull toward you. This gives a broader gap between the two rows of stitching.

FLAT SQUARE STITCH

This is a lovely stitch often used for borders. To work, come up at *A*, down at *B*, and out at *C*. Go back down to *B* (*D*) and diagonally across to *E*. From *E* go back to *A* and then out again at *E*. Continue working along the row making squares.

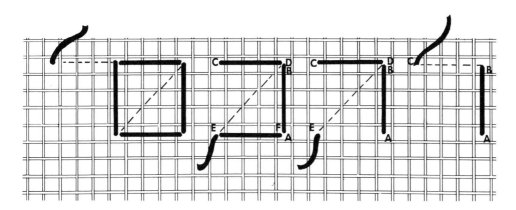

RAISED SQUARE STITCH

This is one of my favorite and most often-used stitches. It is beautiful as a single row, and when worked in rows side by side it resembles gingham. It is often called four-sided stitch. Working from right to left, follow the letters on the diagram, pulling very tightly. A cross with a double arm is formed on the wrong side. This double arm raises the stitch.

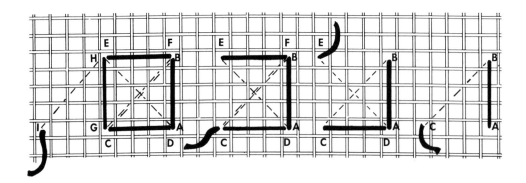

CHAINED BORDER STITCH

This stitch produces a fairly heavy line with large holes along the center. It is worked from left to right over an *even* number of holes, pulled fairly tightly.

It is usually worked in two rows side by side, the second row starting at the dot shown on the diagram. When it is worked in more than two rows it forms a heavy filling. Try it leaving one row between each of the two rows.

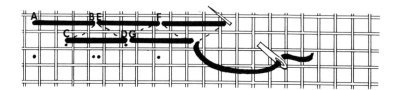

BACKSTITCH

An easy stitch worked from right to left. Do not pull too tightly. To give a heavier line effect make each stitch double.

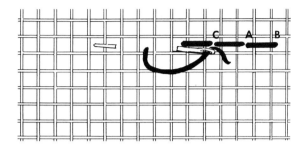

BACKSTITCH VARIATION

Work from right to left. Come up at *A* and down at *B*. Repeat this movement. Then go diagonally up to *C* and down to *D*. From *D* go over to *A'*. From *A* work back again to *D* and diagonally down to *E*. Continue along, alternating the vertical line from up to down.

If you work this stitch as a filling, make the vertical stitches touch so as to produce an open, airy effect.

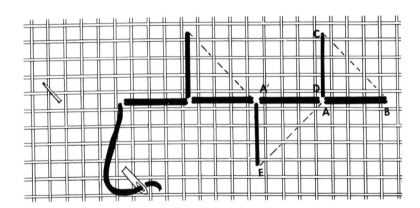

THREE-SIDED STITCH

Pull this stitch very tightly, making triangles with their points alternately up and down. This is a little difficult to work at first but is a very useful stitch for forming a heavy line with large holes.

Work from right to left as follows: Come up at *A* and down at *B*, four threads to the right. Repeat, bringing the needle out at *A*. Go down at *C*, four threads up and two threads to the right. Come out again at *A* and back down at *C*. From *C* come out at *D*, from *D* go down to *A* and back to *D*. Repeat.

1.
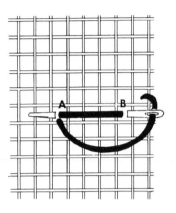

2.
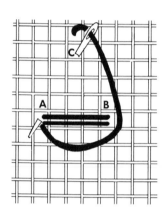

3.
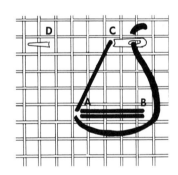

4.
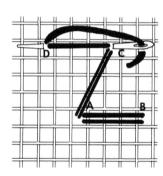

5.
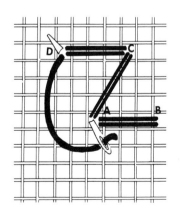

6.
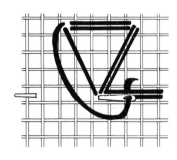

RINGED BACKSTITCH

A lovely stitch often used for borders. Each stitch is worked twice from right to left, in two stages. The first stage makes alternating half-circles.

Follow the diagram and make a row of circles. Pull each stitch very tightly. You will note that on the return journey, the second stage, there will be four *vertical* stitches in the same hole.

If you work only the first stage of this stitch it is called *waved backstitch*.

1.

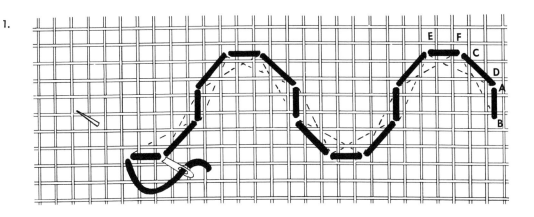

2.

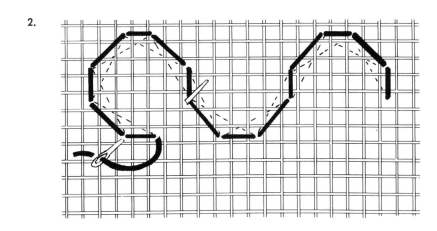

DOUBLE BACKSTITCH

This stitch is the basis for many fillings, such as ripple stitch. Pull it tightly, following the diagram. A herringbone stitch is formed on the wrong side. Work the stitch from right to left.

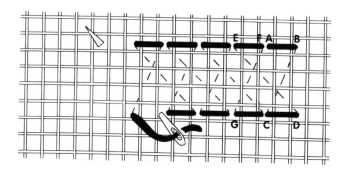

Line Stitches Worked Diagonally

Working on the diagonal is a little more difficult than working on the straight thread, because when the stitches are pulled tightly, the diagonal threads are harder to count. If you find it difficult to count diagonally, count vertically and then horizontally as follows: diagonal four would be up four threads, then across four threads. Practice makes it easier.

DIAGONAL SATIN STITCH

This needs no explanation as it is easy to do once a few stitches are worked.

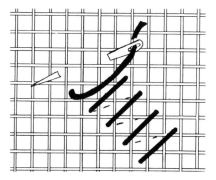

DIAGONAL RAISED SQUARE STITCH

This stitch is as lovely to work diagonally as it is horizontally and is worked in the same way diagonally as horizontally, the only difference being when moving from one square to another. This is clearly shown on the right of the diagram.

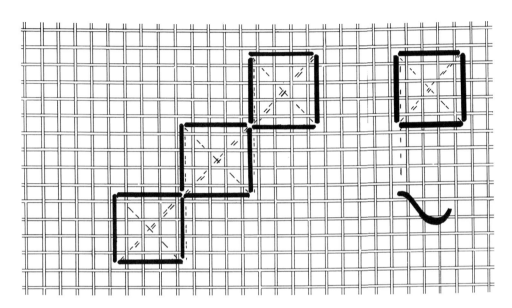

DIAGONAL CHAINED BORDER

This is a little more difficult when worked diagonally than when worked on the horizontal and is most clearly explained by the diagrams.

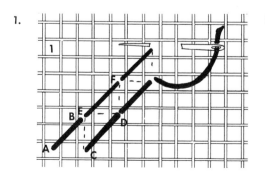

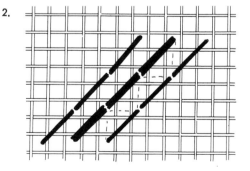

DIAGONAL BACKSTITCH

When this stitch is worked diagonally, the holes formed are more defined and the line is heavier. It is easy to work following the diagram.

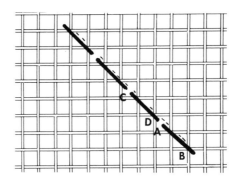

DIAGONAL THREE-SIDED STITCH

Once you understand how to work this stitch horizontally it is not so difficult to work diagonally. The counting on the diagonal may be confusing at first, as the stitch is worked over fewer threads to produce the correct scale. Look at the diagram carefully and practice this stitch on your sampler until you feel completely comfortable with it.

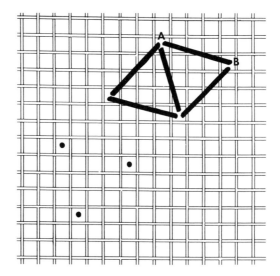

DIAGONAL RINGED BACKSTITCH

The rings of the diagonal ringed backstitch share a diagonal side of the shape instead of a horizontal side. Work the stitch downward in two stages. The first part of the stitch is known as *diagonal waved backstitch*.

1.

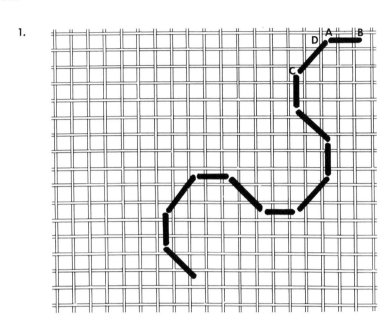

2.

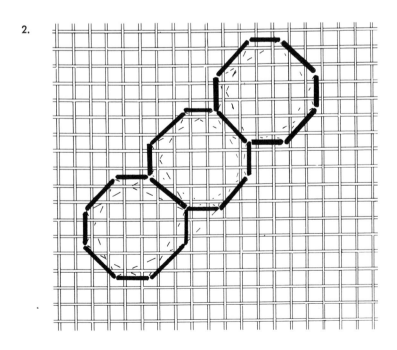

SINGLE FAGGOT STITCH

Pull this stitch very tightly when working. It is one of the simplest stitches and is rarely used in a single row. When two rows are worked, squares are formed. Rows and rows worked together make a delicate, light filling.

Work the stitches downward in steps. Diagonal stitches are formed on the wrong side.

Double faggot stitch is worked in exactly the same manner as the preceding stitch; however, each stitch is worked as a double stitch. It is very effective worked over two threads of the fabric.

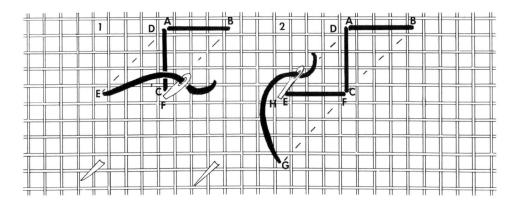

REVERSED FAGGOT STITCH

Work from the bottom left-hand corner to the top right-hand corner. Pull very tightly and large holes will be formed. When this stitch

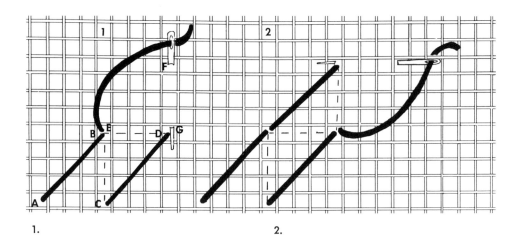

1.   2.

is worked in rows, a very heavy filling with a definite diagonal direction results.

INDIAN DRAWN GROUND STITCH

This stitch works better on fine linen than on canvas. Bring the needle out at *A* and down at *B*. Come out at *C* and down again at *D*. From *D* come out again at *A*, then go back down to *B* and out at *C*. You are now ready to begin the next stitch. From *C* go down to *E*, four threads to the left, and come out at *F*. When one row is completed the work may be turned upside down and more rows worked, thus making a lacy, delicate filling.

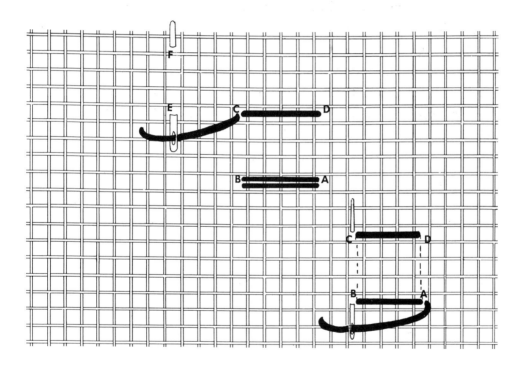

FILLINGS

FILLINGS form the characteristics of pulled thread work, creating the lovely lacy appearance. Therefore, great care must be taken to choose suitable fillings. The inexperienced worker sometimes makes the mistake of using too many fillings on one piece of work. It is more elegant to use fewer fillings.

As fillings have different effects, such as light or dark, lacy or heavy, it is important to select the correct filling to give an even balance to the design.

When planning a design, shade dark and light areas with a pencil. These areas will then correspond to heavy fillings and lacy fillings. For example, the rose design on page 111 has lighter fillings for the petals and heavier ones for the leaves.

Fillings are classified in the same way as the stitches: *horizontal*, *vertical*, and *diagonal*.

The directions have already been given in the previous chapters for working the stitches. Now you must practice making them in rows, thus forming the fillings. (See page 18 for working in rows.)

Fillings Worked Horizontally and Vertically

The arrow on many diagrams indicates where to begin the rows.

RUNNING STITCH FILLING

This is one of the easiest fillings, and when it is stitched, the straight lines on the diagram become more diagonal, as shown in the photograph. A light effect is achieved by pulling tightly.

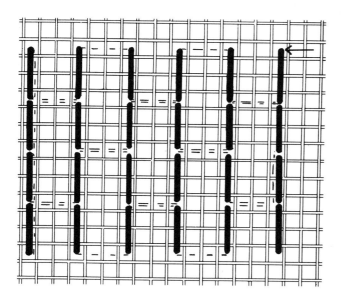

Running stitch filling.

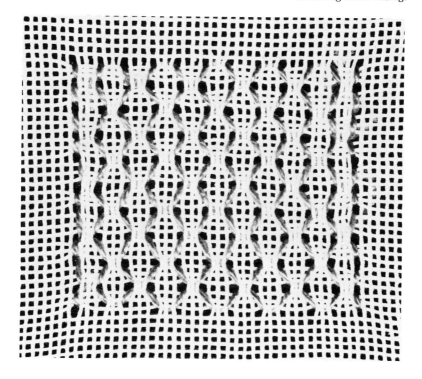

WAVE STITCH FILLING

Wave stitch is worked horizontally from right to left and must be pulled very tightly, producing large holes and making a light, airy appearance. Wave stitch is a very simple stitch, forming the basis for other fillings such as window filling.

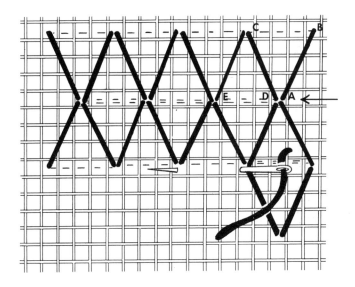

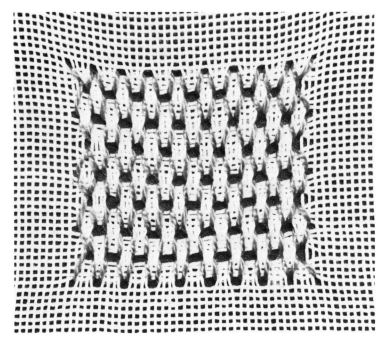

Wave stitch filling.

WINDOW FILLING

As mentioned, window filling is a form of wave filling, the only difference being that one thread of the fabric is left between each stitch and each row, giving a more defined pattern. This is a beautiful filling with a very lacy effect. For an even more lacy effect, leave two threads between each stitch and row, making *double window filling*. For both fillings turn the work around to start the second row (see *M* on diagram), working always from right to left.

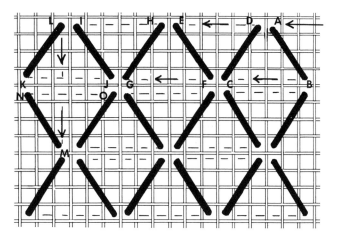

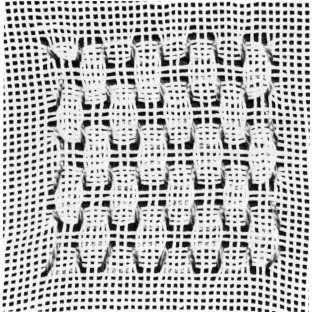

Double window filling.

Window filling.

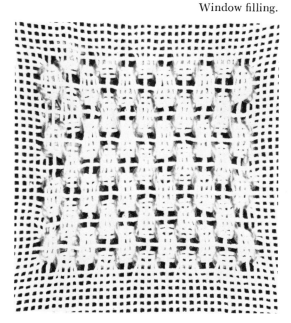

REVERSE WAVE STITCH FILLING

This is the reverse side of wave stitch. Horizontal lines are formed on the right side of the work.

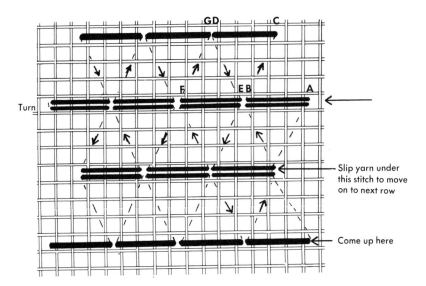

DOUBLE STITCH FILLING

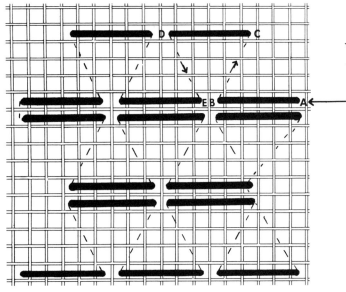

This is the reverse side of window filling stitch, producing the same lacy effect.

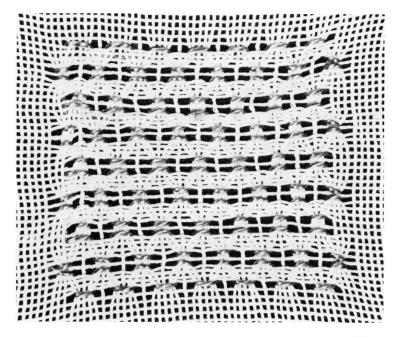

Double stitch filling.

COIL STITCH FILLING

A very simple stitch giving a medium lacy effect. You must pull very tightly when stitching to get the best effect. Work in rows from right to left, turning the work at the end of each row.

Coil stitch filling.

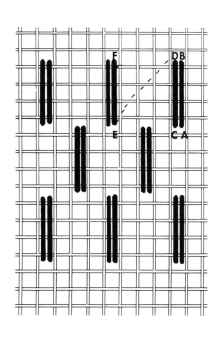

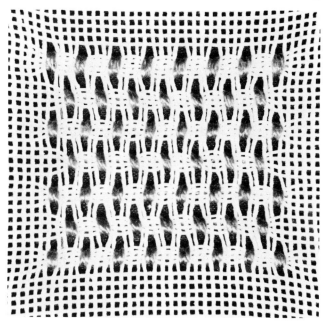

PEBBLE STITCH FILLING

This is an easy stitch to work and is worked in rows. Each row is worked in two stages. Pull each stitch very hard. The diagram shows clearly how to work the stitches.

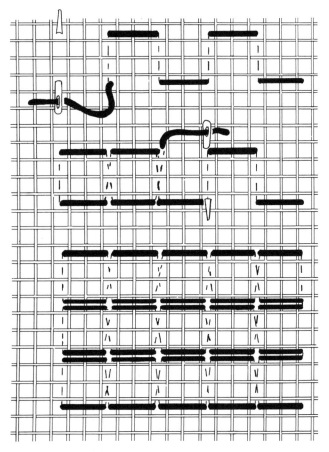

1.

2.

3.

Pebble stitch filling.

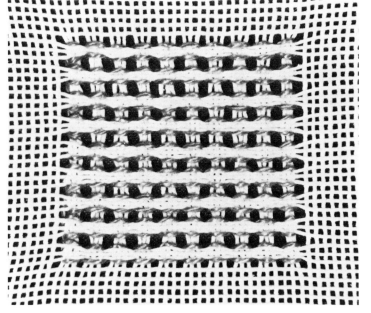

COBBLER STITCH FILLING

Begin at the arrow on the diagram and work along the row as shown. For the second row skip two threads of the fabric and repeat the first row. Fill the whole surface to be worked in this manner before working the second stage of the stitch.

For the second stage, turn the canvas and work horizontally, again in rows, making boxes, each with two threads in between. The finished effect of this stitch is similar to double window filling, but a more defined pattern results.

1.

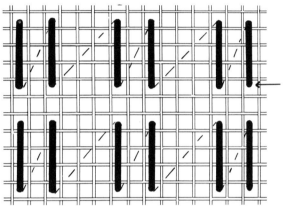

2.

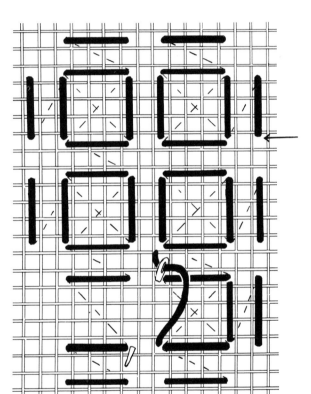

Cobbler stitch filling.

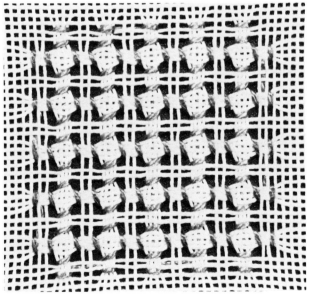

FRAMED CROSS FILLING

This is made by altering the count of cobbler filling to four and one, instead of four and two threads. Leave one thread between each row.

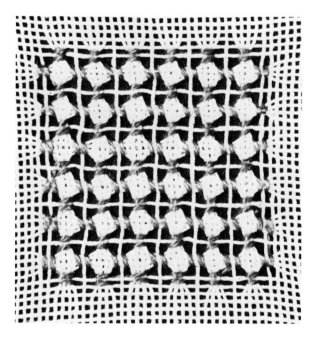

Framed cross filling.

PUNCH STITCH FILLING

This is exactly the same as the preceding stitch, but no threads are left between rows, thus giving a heavier effect.

1.

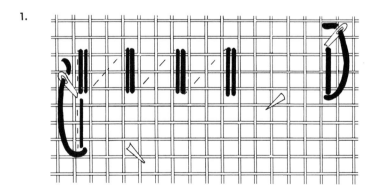

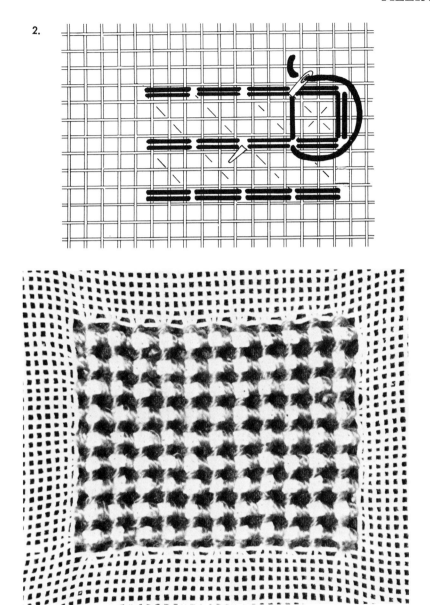

Punch stitch filling.

HONEYCOMB FILLING

A very popular stitch giving a rough texture. I love working this stitch, and as you can see in the photograph, it changes when stitched to look more diagonal. It looks best in a heavy yarn pulled very tightly.

To work, come up at *A* and down at *B*, then out at *C*. From *C* go back to *B* (*D*) and come out again at *C* (*E*). To begin the second row, see diagram 2. As you work the second row you will notice that you are doubling all the vertical stitches.

1.

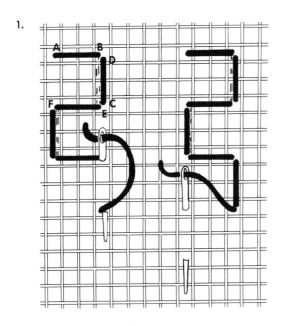

2.

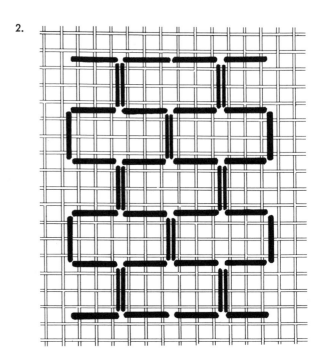

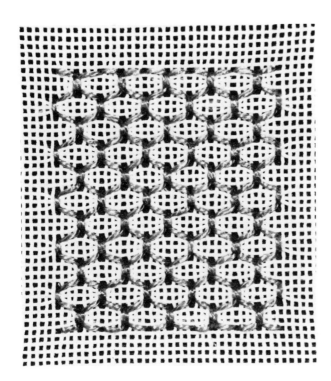

Honeycomb filling.

RAISED SQUARE STITCH FILLING

This filling is made by working rows of raised square stitch side by side. It gives a good, heavy effect and is simple to work. (See raised square stitch on page 23.)

Raised square stitch filling.

RINGED BACKSTITCH FILLING

This stitch is a filling worked in rows of ringed backstitch. For working see ringed backstitch on page 27. This stitch gives a lovely open effect and is shown to its full advantage over large areas.

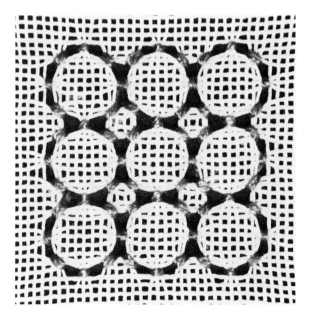

Ringed backstitch filling.

FESTOON STITCH FILLING

This stitch is a variation of waved backstitch and has a definite movement in its effect. Again, it needs a fairly large area to be appreciated.

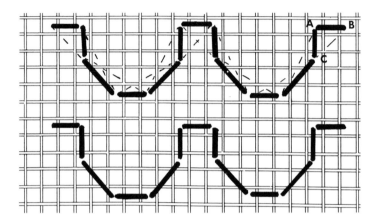

GREEK CROSS STITCH FILLING

Greek cross stitch is an easy stitch based on the blanket stitch. The diagram shows how to work the stitch in five steps. Diagram 5

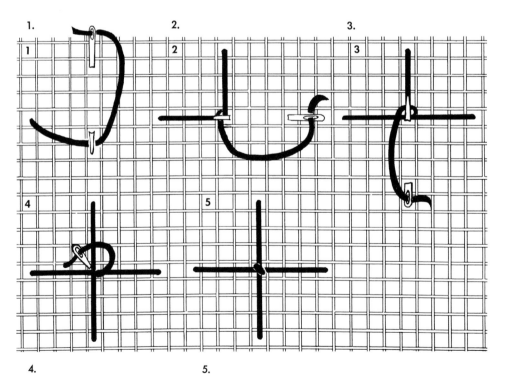

shows the finished stitch. The small graphs *A* through *D* show the spacing of the Greek crosses in different ways to form lacy fillings.

Greek cross stitch fillings need large areas to be most effective. They work very well as backgrounds of designs.

A.

B.

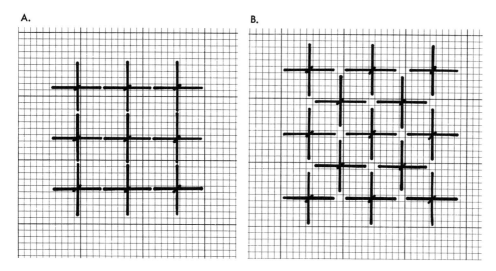

Greek cross stitch filling.

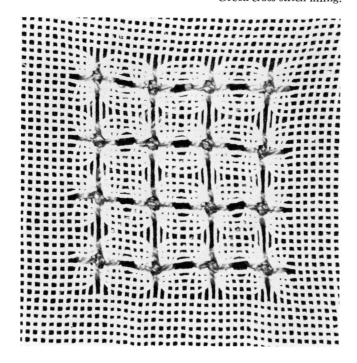

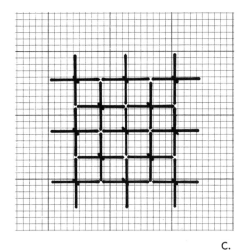

C.

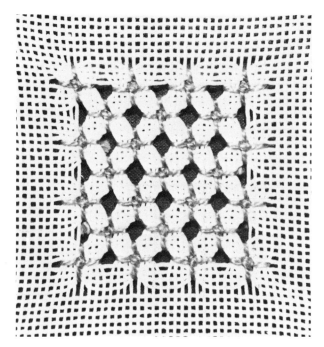

Greek cross stitch filling.

Greek cross stitch filling.

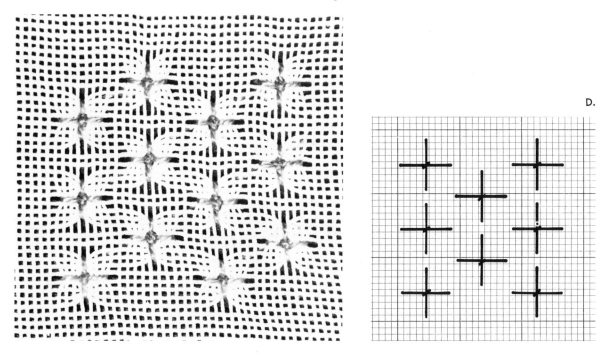

D.

CROSS STITCH VARIATION FILLING

This filling is based on the cross stitch and is worked in two stages. It is very easy to stitch and the result is a heavy, textured stitch. Pull very tightly. It is easy to stitch by following the two diagrams.

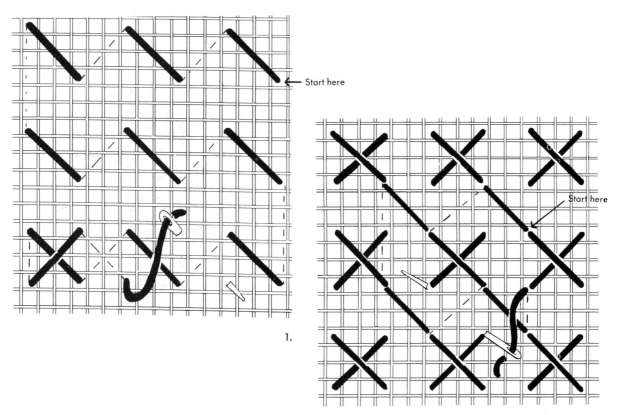

1.

2.

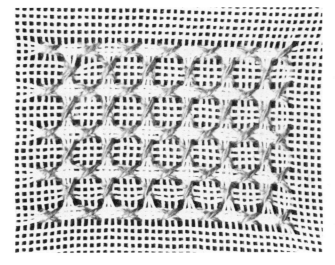

Cross stitch variation filling.

MOSAIC STITCH FILLING

I love the effect of this stitch and use it in both single units and fillings. It gives a very delicate, lacy effect and is so easy to work. First work the satin stitches over four threads, then the four-sided stitch, and last a cross stitch. This is one of the few pulled work stitches that works well in a contrasting color.

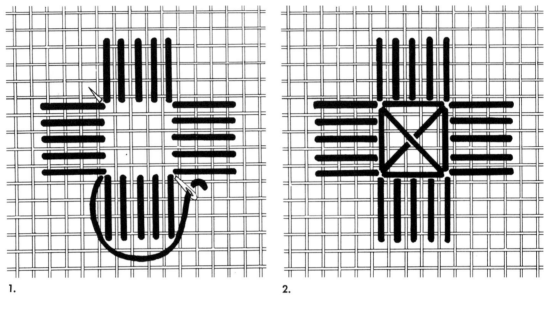

1.   2.

Mosaic stitch filling.

DRAWN SQUARE FILLING

A satin stitch square worked over two threads. The square is worked first as shown in the diagram, then the eyelet is worked in the center. All the stitches should be pulled very tightly. A hole is formed in the middle of the eyelet. A very solid filling is formed. It can be worked in two colors, the satin stitch square in a darker color than the eyelet. This is a beautiful filling to stitch.

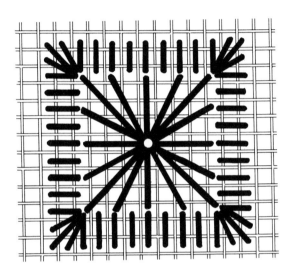

Drawn square filling.

MALTESE FILLING

This is another heavy filling worked in satin stitch in a similar way to mosaic filling, except that the satin stitches are worked over two stitches instead of four. It takes concentration to keep the count correct, although the stitches themselves are easy to work.

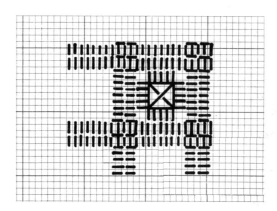

Maltese filling.

FRAMED EYELET FILLING

To make this filling, combine raised square stitch with eyelet stitch. First work a row of raised square stitches horizontally (see page

23), then a row of eyelets (see page 86), placing each eyelet four threads apart. Work another horizontal row of raised square stitch, then eyelet again. When you have worked all the rows of raised square stitch and eyelets, turn the work around and fill in the four threads left between each eyelet with raised square stitch. This filling gives a very open, lacy effect and is fun to stitch.

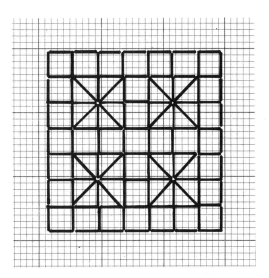

Framed eyelet filling.

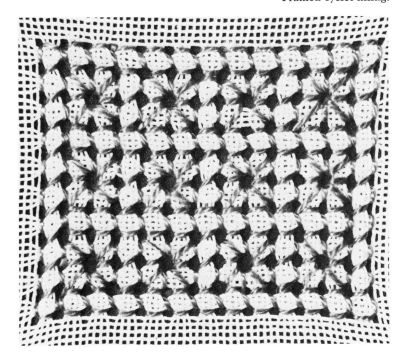

STEP STITCH FILLING

Step stitch filling and the next eight fillings are all based on satin stitch and are suitable for covering large shapes and areas. The tighter the stitch is pulled, the more lacy the filling becomes. For best results the step stitch should be worked diagonally across the fabric, starting at

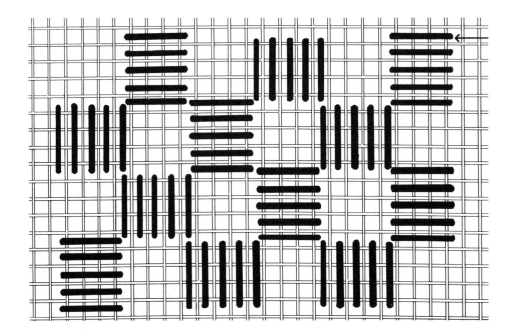

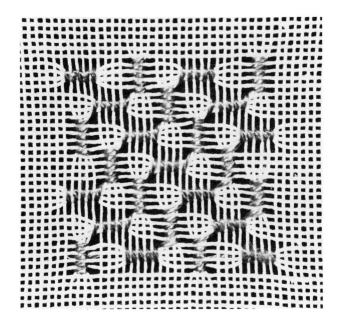

Step stitch filling.

the arrow on the diagram. If you do not wish to pull the satin stitch tightly, I suggest that you work with a thicker yarn to give a very solid effect.

CHESSBOARD FILLING

This is one of my favorite satin stitch fillings with many uses. It is very lovely when worked with a fine yarn pulled tightly.

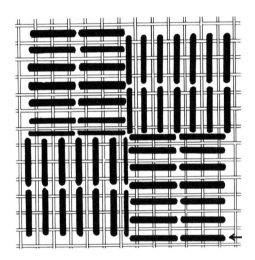

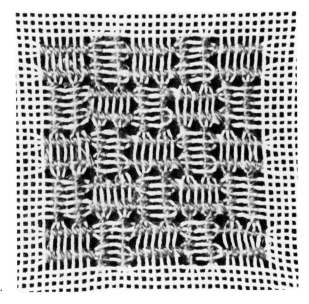

Chessboard filling.

SMALL CHESSBOARD FILLING

A similar filling to the preceding one, only giving a more dainty effect.

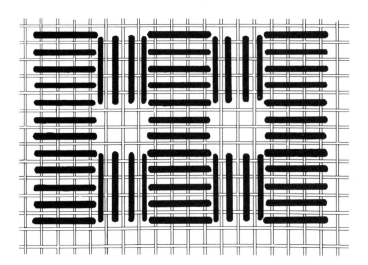

Small chessboard filling.

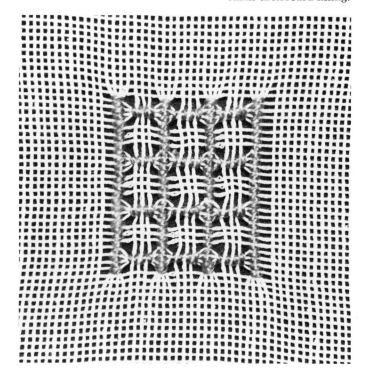

OPEN BASKET FILLING

A lacy, basket-like effect is produced by this filling. A little concentration is needed to make the "basket" appearance but is well worth
the time as it is so beautiful.

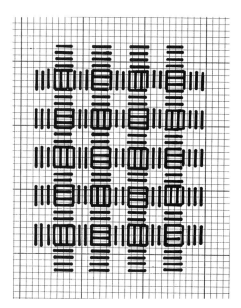

Open basket filling.

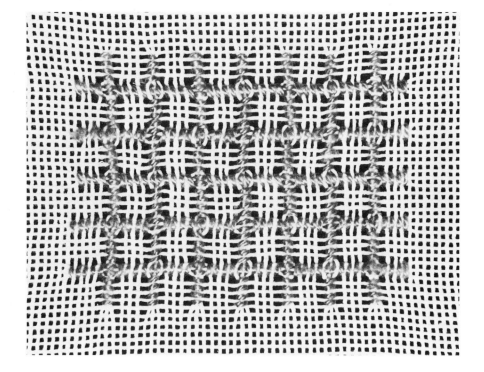

ALGERIAN FILLING

This should be stitched on the diagonal on a fine fabric for the best effect. On a coarser fabric a heavy, solid filling results.

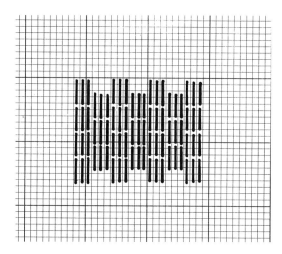

Algerian filling.

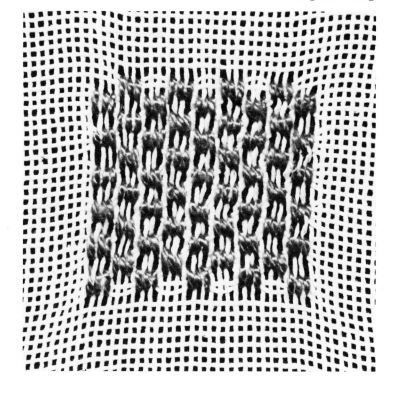

GOBELIN FILLING

A heavy satin stitch filling worked in horizontal rows.

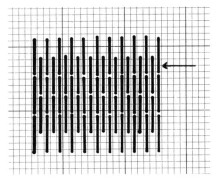

MOSAIC DIAMOND FILLING

Mosaic diamond filling gives a very heavy effect and works best in a fine yarn. I find it easier to work rows 1, 3, and 5 first, and then fill in the diamonds in the spaces left.

Mosaic diamond filling.

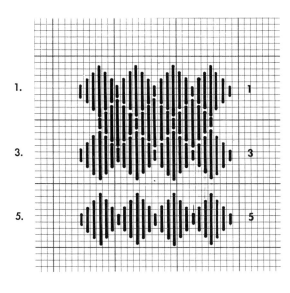

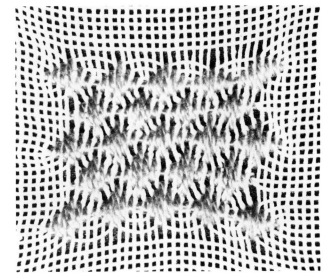

SATIN STITCH FILLING

Satin stitch filling should be worked very tightly to produce a diamond shape. This certainly is a charming filling when worked in an all-over pattern with a fine yarn. Diagram 2 shows the arrangement of blocks to make the all-over filling.

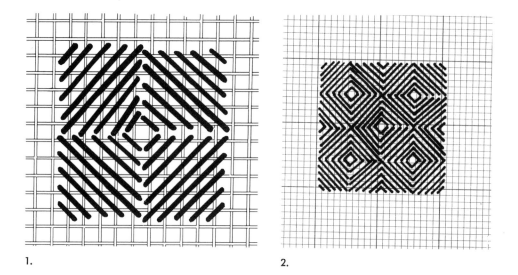

1.   2.

LOZENGE FILLING

A very large area is needed to show this satin stitch filling to its best advantage. It works very well as an all-over design for a pillow or

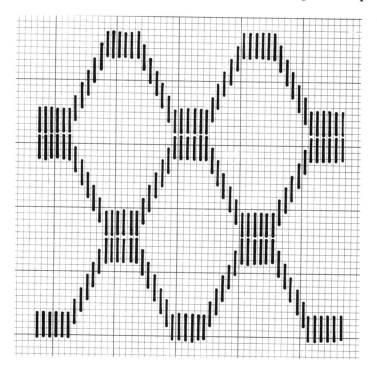

tablecloth. This is very easy to stitch. For a different effect try adding single eyelets in the center of each open space. Lozenge filling has a lot of possibilities for experimenting. When working this pattern do not pull too tightly.

Lozenge filling.

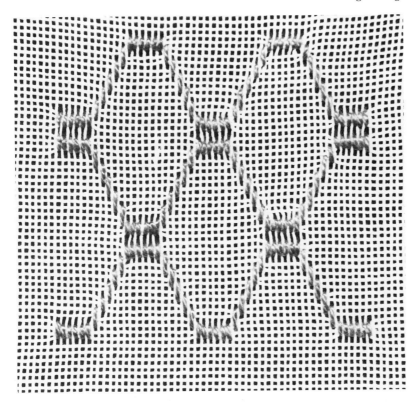

BRAID STITCH FILLING

Braid stitch filling and the following six fillings are all a variation of the double backstitch. All these patterns need a large area to be most appreciated and should be stitched on a soft fabric such as linen, rather than canvas. It is much easier to work these fillings on a frame. As most of the patterns have long threads on the wrong side, they are not suitable for practical items such as napkins but work well as backgrounds for pillows and wall hangings.

Braid stitch filling has a lot of movement when stitched and care must be taken to count the pattern correctly so that the second row is placed in the correct position in relation to the first. Begin at the arrow and work horizontally from right to left, turning the work at the end of each row.

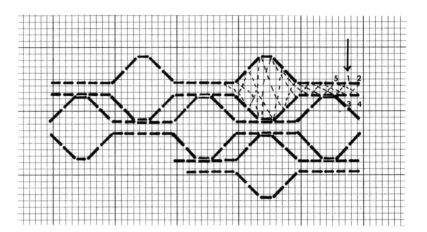

CUSHION FILLING

Cushion filling gets its name from the cushion-like ovals produced by pulling the double backstitches very tightly. This pattern can be worked on smaller areas than the braid stitch.

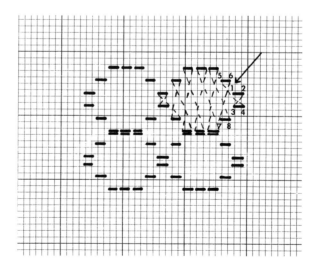

DIAMOND FILLING

You can work the diamonds with more or fewer steps, depending on the area to be filled. This is a fun filling to work; it needs a large area to be appreciated. At the end of each row, turn the work so that you always work from right to left.

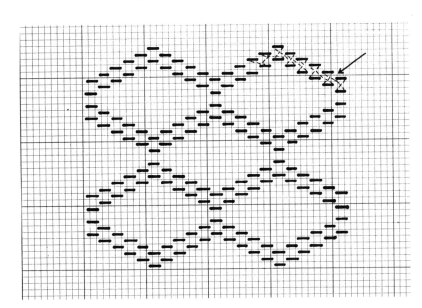

Diamond filling.

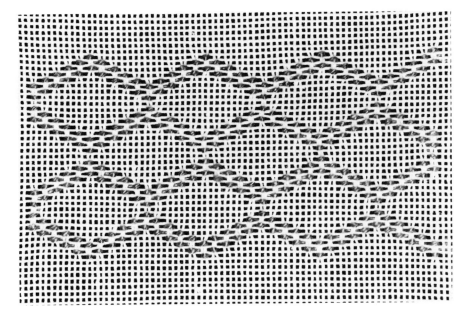

FINNISH STITCH FILLING

Another double backstitch filling worked in steps on the diagonal; you will note that double stitches are made where the steps meet. An easy filling to stitch by following the diagram carefully.

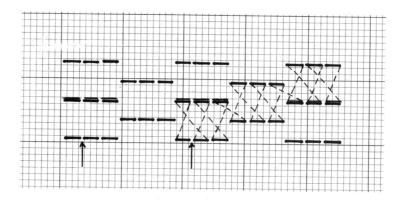

Finnish stitch filling.

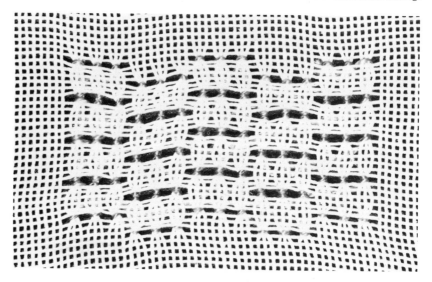

RIPPLE STITCH FILLING

Ripple stitch needs a very large area to stand out. It is made up of alternate blocks of double backstitch. Each row fits into the spaces left between the blocks of the previous row.

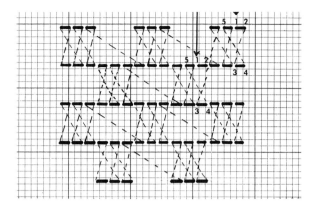

SQUARE STITCH FILLING

The effect of this stitch is neat, box-like shapes evenly spaced. The squares are alternated to make a lacy pattern. Work the double backstitch around the shape beginning at opposite corners and stitching in a clockwise direction.

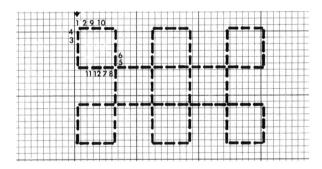

TRIANGLE STITCH FILLING

Work this stitch in diagonal rows, as clearly shown in the diagram. Take care in placing each row.

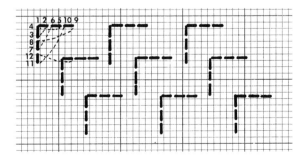

Fillings Worked Diagonally

The following fillings work best when stitched diagonally. However, any worker finding it easier to stitch some of the fillings on the horizontal or vertical may do so. Both step stitch filling and Algerian filling, for example, can be worked diagonally but for purposes of classification were described in the preceding section.

SINGLE FAGGOT FILLING

Work this filling from the top right to the bottom left of the piece. Single faggot filling is one of the easiest of all the diagonal stitches. Work rows of single faggot stitch (page 32) side by side, turning the work at the end of each row. This gives a very lacy, open filling.

Single faggot filling.

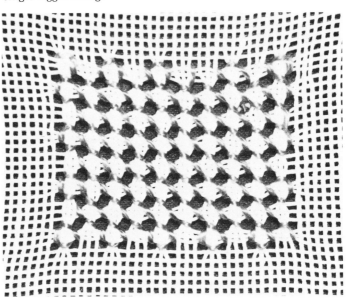

REVERSED FAGGOT FILLING

Reversed faggot filling is worked from the bottom left to the top right of the work. Turn the work to begin each new row. Follow the diagram on page 32 for reversed faggot stitch. A very open effect is achieved.

Reversed faggot filling.

DOUBLE FAGGOT FILLING

Double faggot filling is worked in exactly the same way as single faggot filling, except that each stitch is worked twice, giving a more solid effect. (See the diagram on page 32.)

Double faggot filling.

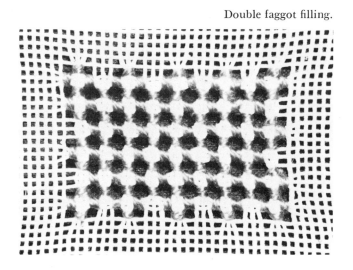

RUSSIAN FILLING

Russian filling consists completely of reversed faggot filling stitch worked first from the bottom left to the top right. When all these rows have been completed, the work is turned around and the second set of rows is worked, using the same holes as those used for the first rows.

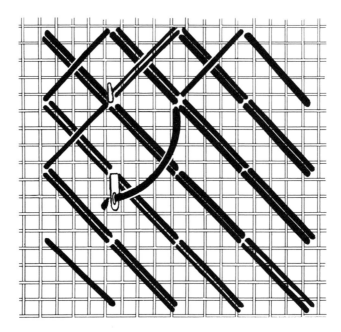

Russian filling.

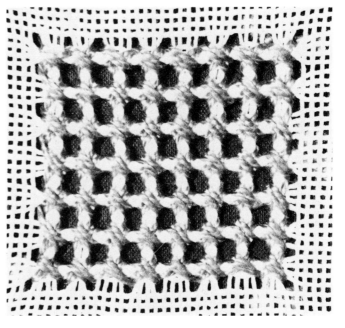

DIAGONAL DRAWN FILLING

An easy filling to stitch, giving a beautiful lacy effect. To work it, stitch rows of single faggot one diagonal thread apart. If more threads are left between the rows of faggoting, a more open effect results.

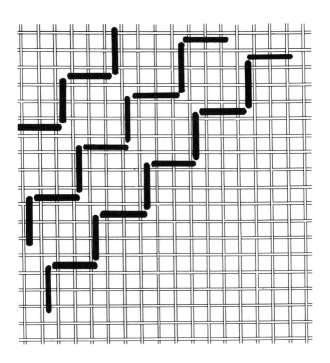

Diagonal drawn filling.

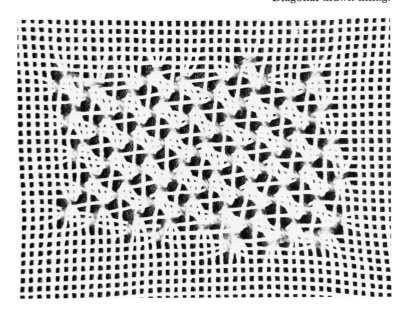

DIAGONAL CHEVRON FILLING

For this filling the rows are worked up and down. First work rows of single faggot stitches over three threads, each spaced three threads apart. Then, between rows, using the same holes, fit a line of reversed faggot. A lacy, intricate effect results.

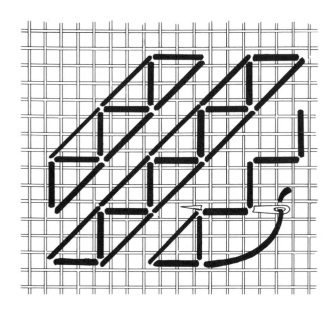

Diagonal chevron filling.

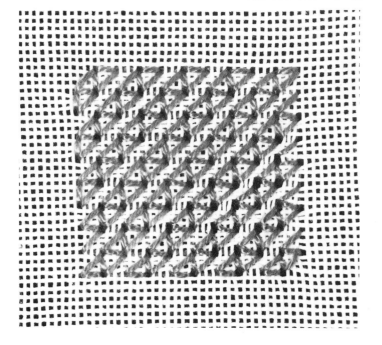

CROSSED FAGGOT FILLING

First work rows of single faggot stitch and then work diagonal cross filling.

Crossed faggot filling.

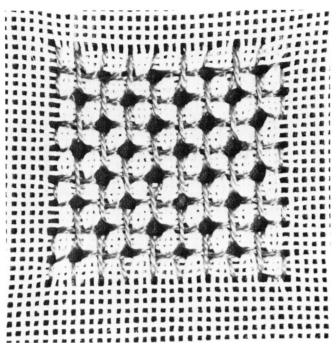

NET FILLING

Net filling is a lovely lacy filling made by combining large and small single faggot stitches together in rows. The diagram explains the simplest way to do the stitch.

When this filling is worked over four threads and two threads it is known as *drawn faggot filling*.

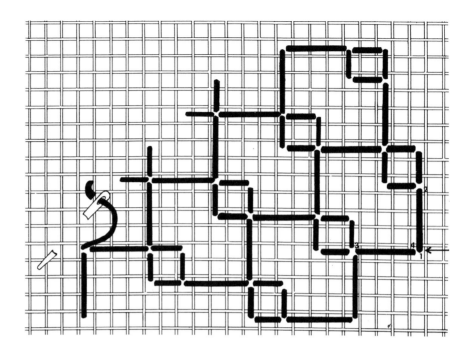

Net filling.

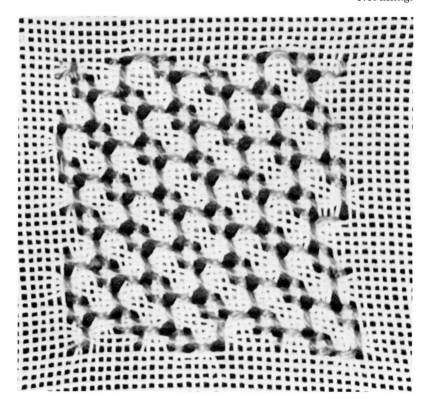

DIAGONAL CROSS FILLING

This is a very easy filling to work and gives a solid, lacy effect. It consists of rows of cross stitches worked close to each other. First work all the half crosses in one row before coming back to complete the crosses. Be sure to pull the stitches very tightly. This stitch is sometimes called *ridge filling*.

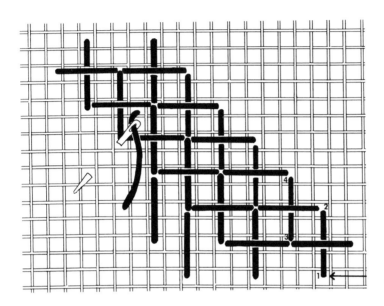

Diagonal cross filling.

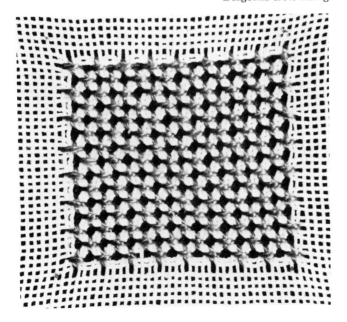

DIAGONAL RAISED BAND FILLING

The bands are worked upward from right to left. First make the vertical stitches upward and then make the horizontal stitches downward, using the same holes as the vertical stitches. Pull these stitches very tightly in order to make the ridges. This filling has a very strong sense of direction and gives a fairly solid effect.

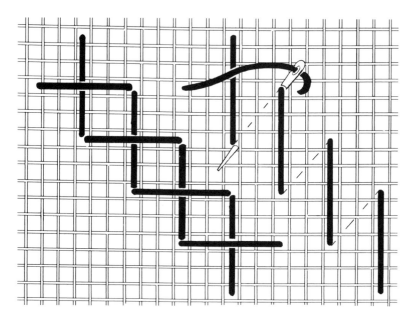

Diagonal raised band filling.

OPEN TRELLIS FILLING

This is an easy, beautiful filling to work. It is made up of a series of diagonal raised bands on top of each other at various intervals to make a trellis-like effect. The diagram shows clearly how to work the filling.

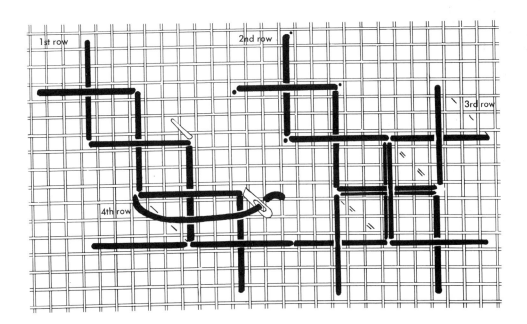

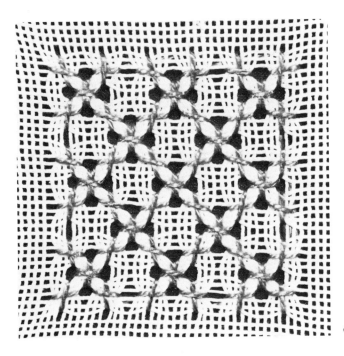

Open trellis filling.

CROSS STITCH CHEVRON FILLING

A very heavy filling produced by working two rows of reversed faggot and then two rows of cross stitch over three threads.

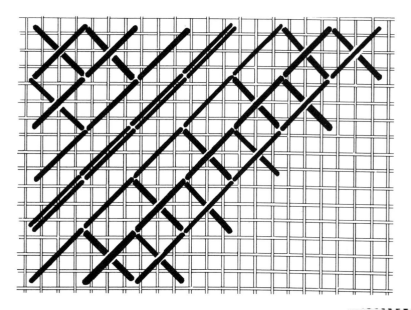

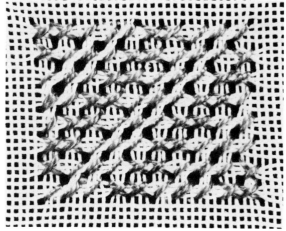

Cross stitch chevron filling.

CHECKER STITCH FILLING

Checker stitch is a lacy filling with a rough texture, which works best when not pulled too tightly. It is worked similarly to open trellis filling, but the cross stitches are elongated.

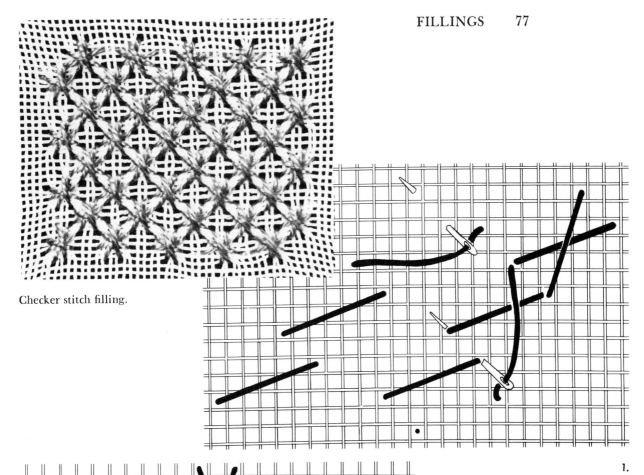

Checker stitch filling.

1.

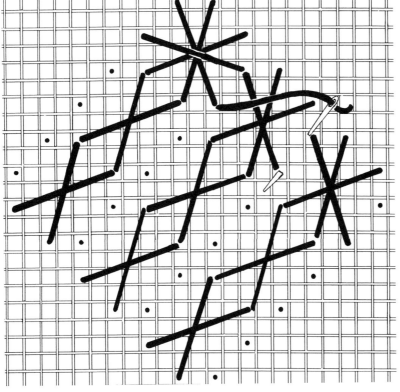

2.

DETACHED SQUARE FILLING

This is a large, airy filling which is a pleasure to stitch. It is worked in two stages. First work all the diagonal stitches in one direction until the whole area is covered (diagram 1). Then work back down the row using the same holes, thus making double stitches (diagram 2).

Then turn the work and complete the squares (diagram 3), linking the ends of the stitches already made.

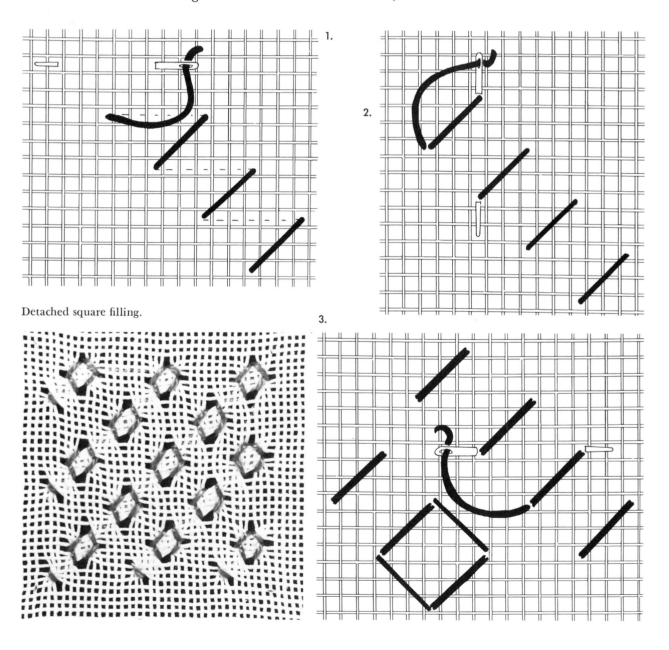

Detached square filling.

DRAWN BUTTONHOLE FILLING

This stitch is a heavy filling worked in rows of blanket stitch on the diagonal. Diagram 1 shows how to work one blanket stitch and diagram 2 shows the placement of the rows to make a filling.

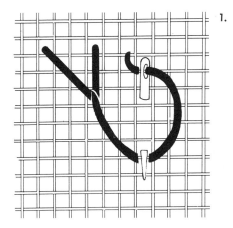
1.

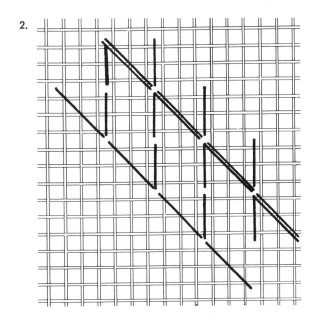
2.

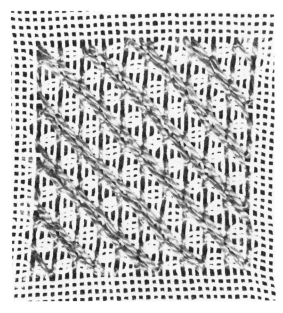

Drawn buttonhole filling.

ROSETTE FILLING

Work the rosettes diagonally, one motif at a time. Pull each stitch tightly to raise the center of each rosette. Follow the diagrams for the simplest method of working the filling.

1.

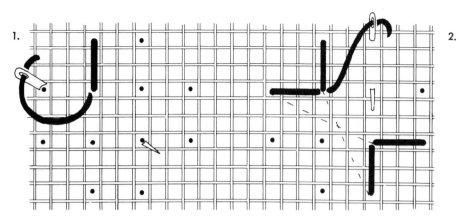

2.

3.

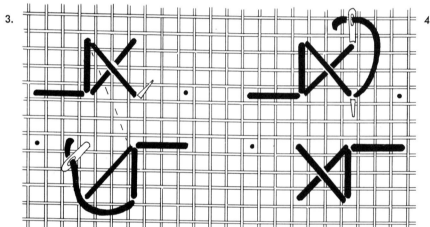

4.

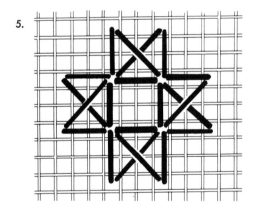

5.

Rosette filling.

POINTED STARS FILLING

A large-scale filling with a starlike appearance. Come up at *A* (this is the center of the star) and down at *B*, then up at *C*. From *C* go back down at *B* and out again at *A*. Then go down at *D* and out again at *C*. From *C* go back in at *D* and out again at *A*. From *A* go in at *E*, out at *C*, and in again at *E*. You have now made one arm of the star. Repeat until four arms are made.

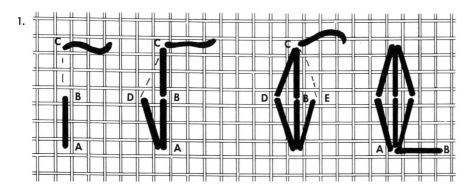

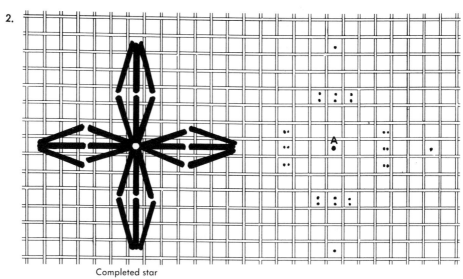

Completed star

Eyelets

Eyelets are some of the most beautiful stitches in pulled thread work. They are basically satin stitches all worked into the same center hole. When pulled tightly a large hole is formed in the center. Always work from the outside of the eyelet to the hole in the center.

Eyelets can be worked as single units, as fillings, or combined with other stitches to form composite fillings. Unlike most pulled thread stitches, they work beautifully in color.

SQUARE EYELETS

The small eyelet in diagram 1 is worked over two threads to the center, and the large eyelet in diagram 2 over four threads. It is sometimes necessary to use a finer yarn when working eyelets to ensure a more even result.

1.

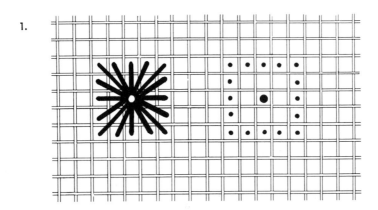

2.

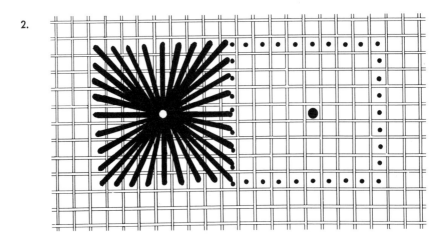

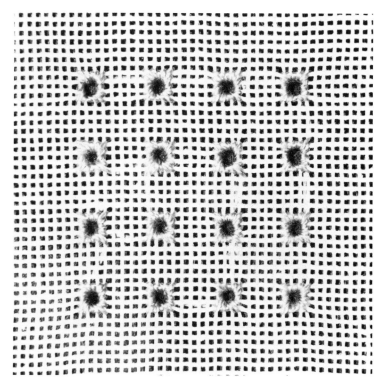

Small eyelet worked over two threads.

Small eyelet worked over four threads.

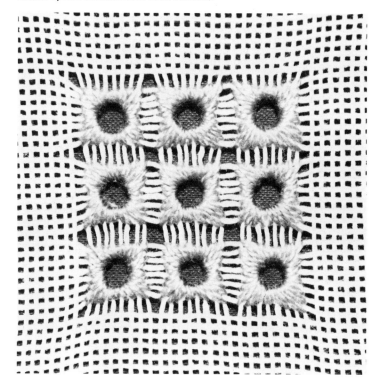

SINGLE CROSS EYELET

A lovely effect is achieved by leaving one thread between each quarter of a square eyelet. A window-like pattern is formed.

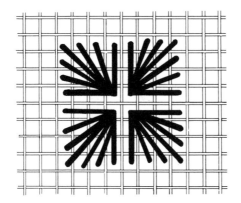

Single-cross eyelet.

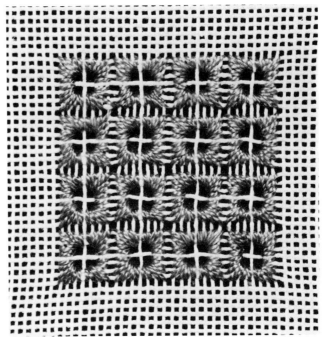

DOUBLE CROSS EYELET

A beautiful eyelet worked similarly to the preceding one except that you leave two threads between each quarter and work one stitch between these two threads. The dot shows where to begin the next eyelet.

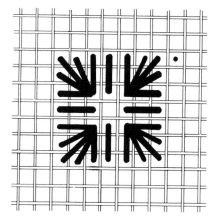

Double-cross eyelet.

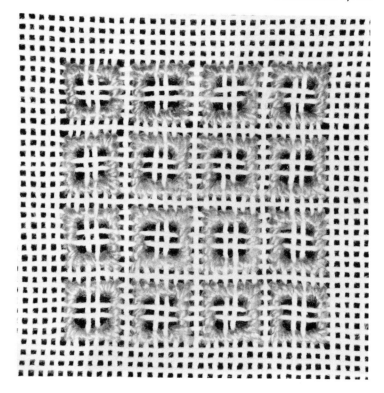

STAR EYELET

Star eyelets are easier when stitched on the diagonal and not pulled too tightly. The diagram clearly shows the working of the eyelets.

Some lovely fillings can be made combining square eyelets with star eyelets.

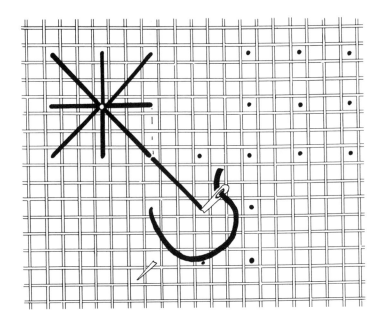

Star eyelet.

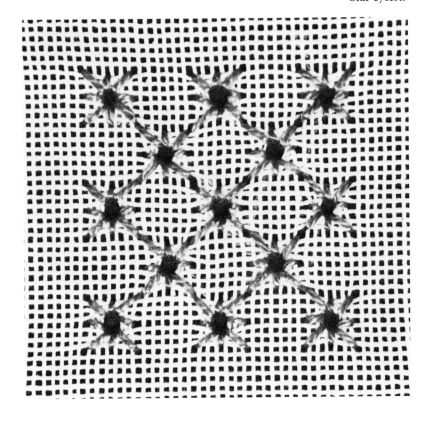

ROUND EYELET

This has softer lines than the star eyelet and is easy to work.

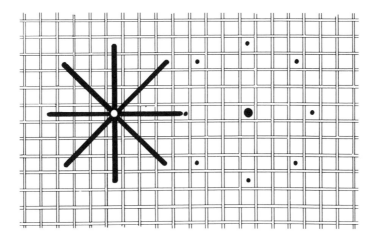

Round eyelet.

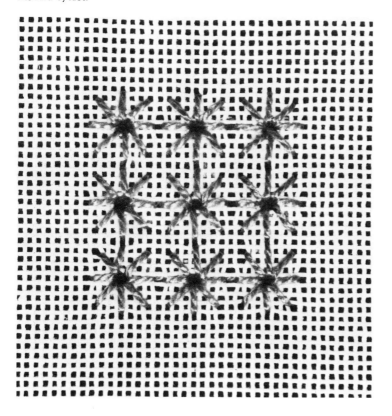

HEXAGONAL EYELET

Each straight stitch of this filling is worked double, to make an open, airy pattern.

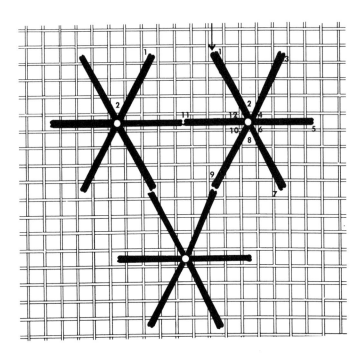

Hexagonal eyelet.

DIAMOND EYELET

A delicate eyelet with many uses. It can be pulled tightly or left flat; either way it looks beautiful. The eyelet in the diagram is worked over ten threads, five each way from the center. See Plate 1.

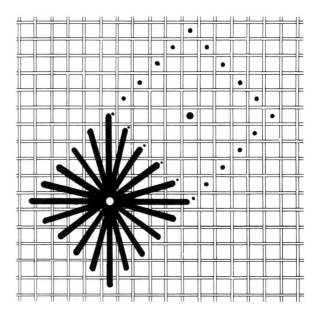

BARRED BUTTONHOLE EYELET

This eyelet is worked in exactly the same way as square eyelet, except that blanket stitch is used instead of satin stitch.

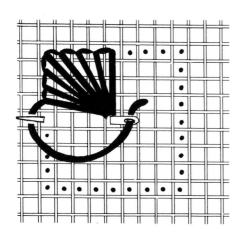

Barred buttonhole eyelet.

ITALIAN EYELET FILLING

A heavy filling worked in star eyelets overlapping each other on the horizontal rows. It is clearly explained by the diagram.

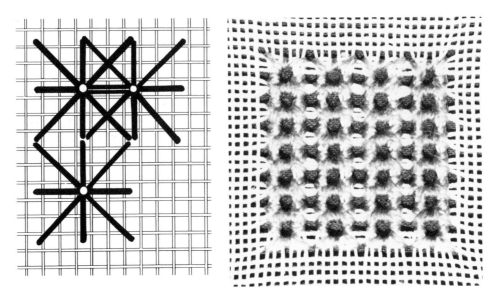

Italian eyelet filling.

EYELET STITCH FILLING

This filling is worked in three-sided stitch and takes a little practice to do. Follow the diagram for one eyelet before attempting the fillings in diagram 2 and diagram 3. Remember, as in three-sided stitch, to work each stitch double.

Eyelet stitch filling.

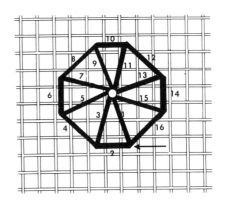

1.

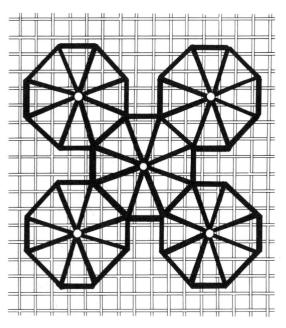

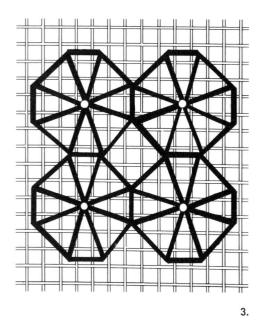

3.

2.

Composite Fillings

These are made up of more than one stitch. Some of the fillings work very well in two colors (see color plates).

SATIN STITCH AND EYELET FILLING

A lovely example of this filling worked in maroon and beige is shown in Plate 2. The filling is pretty as an all-over design for a pillow cover or handbag.

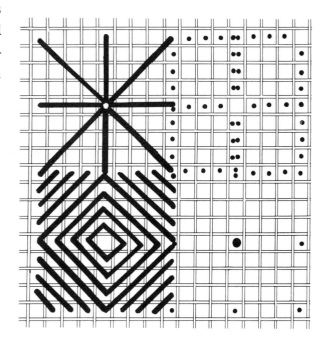

OUTLINED DIAMOND FILLING

The easiest way to stitch the filling is to work the diagonal satin stitches first and then fill in the areas formed with diamond eyelets. See Plate 3.

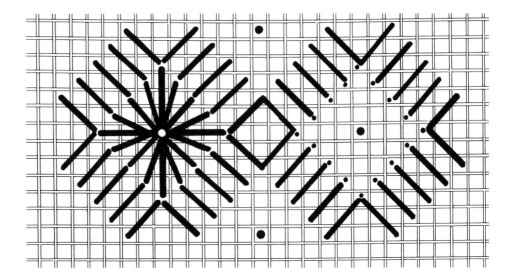

Outlined diamond filling.

EYELET AND STEP STITCH FILLING

This is such fun to stitch, with beautiful results. Work all the steps first in satin stitch, then add the square eyelets. A lovely filling for an all-over pattern for the yoke of a blouse or a lacy pillow. See Plate 4.

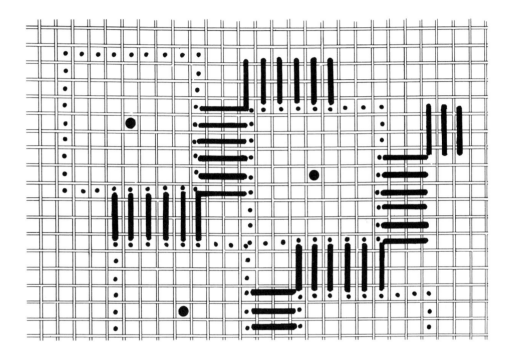

OUTLINED SQUARE EYELET FILLING

A very lacy effect is achieved by this filling. Stitch all the diagonal satin stitches first and then place the square eyelets in the centers, each over two threads. See Plate 5.

SQUARE EYELET AND SATIN STITCH FILLING

A heavy, solid effect is made by this combination. The eyelets are worked after all the satin stitches are made. This filling is similar to mosaic filling. See Plate 6.

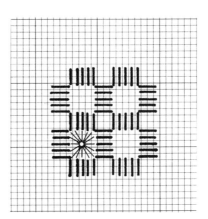

SATIN STITCH BLOCKS WITH FOUR-SIDED STITCH

Little explanation is needed to work this filling. The easiest way is first to work all the four-sided stitch blocks on the diagonal. Then fill in the satin stitch blocks. See Plate 7.

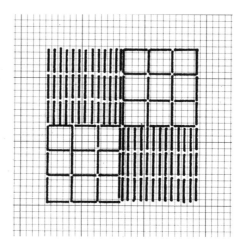

SATIN STITCH ALTERNATING WITH FOUR-SIDED STITCH

A row of satin stitch is worked over three threads, then three rows of four-sided stitches over four threads, alternating the boxes. This sequence is repeated to form a filling. See Plate 8.

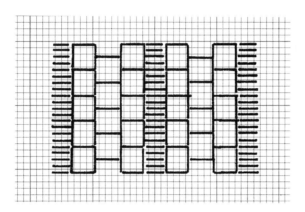

SATIN STITCH WITH FOUR-SIDED STITCH

One four-sided stitch is worked over four threads, then four satin stitches, then one four-sided stitch, then four satin stitches. Continue in this way along the row. For the second row, alternate the stitches. It is clearly shown in the diagram. See Plate 9.

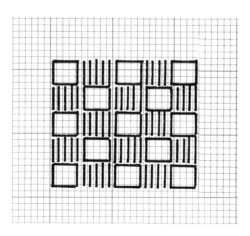

HONEYCOMB SATIN STITCH FILLING

The easiest way to work this filling is first to stitch all the satin stitches over three threads, leaving six threads between each row. Then in the six threads work two rows of honeycomb stitch. The effect is beautiful in color. See Plate 10.

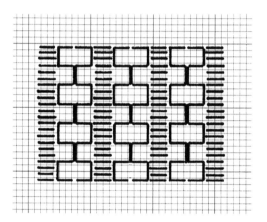

THICKET FILLING

Small eyelet squares are worked over four threads alternating with five satin stitches over two threads. On the second row the eyelets are spaced beneath the satin stitches. See Plate 11.

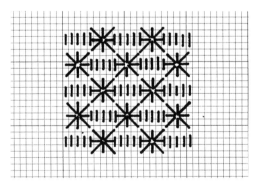

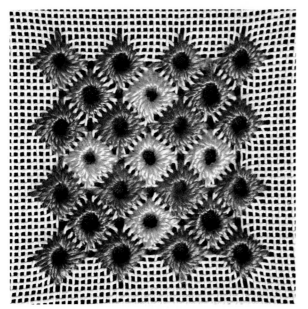

Plate 1. Diamond eyelet filling.

Plate 2. Satin stitch and eyelet filling.

Plate 3. Outlined diamond filling.

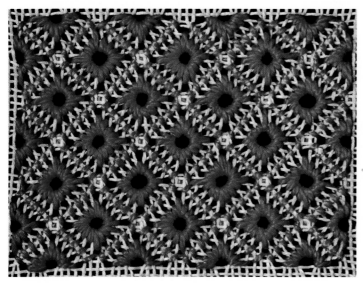

Plate 4. Eyelet and step stitch filling.

Plate 5. Outlined square eyelet filling.

Plate 6. Square eyelet and satin stitch filling.

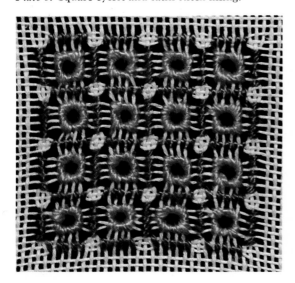

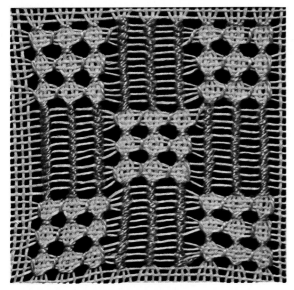

Plate 7. Satin stitch blocks with four-sided stitch.

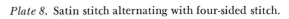
Plate 8. Satin stitch alternating with four-sided stitch.

Plate 9. Satin stitch with four-sided stitch.

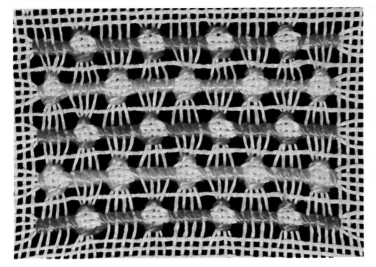

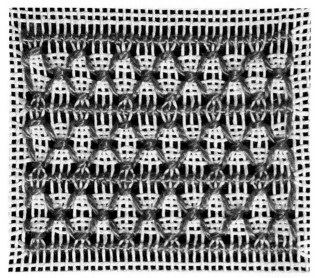

Plate 10. Honeycomb and satin stitch filling.

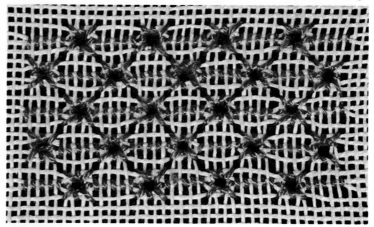

Plate 11. Thicket filling.

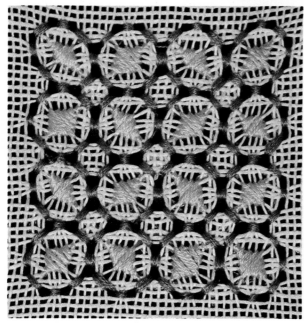

Plate 12. Ringed backstitch with satin stitch.

Plate 13. Diamond and spot filling.

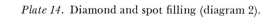
Plate 14. Diamond and spot filling (diagram 2).

Plate 15. Greek cross and satin stitch filling.

Plate 16. Square stitch with satin stitch filling.

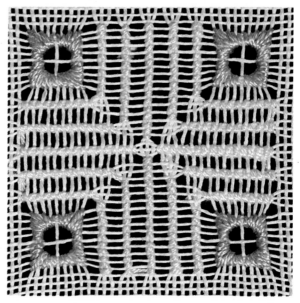

Plate 17. Single cross eyelet with satin stitch.

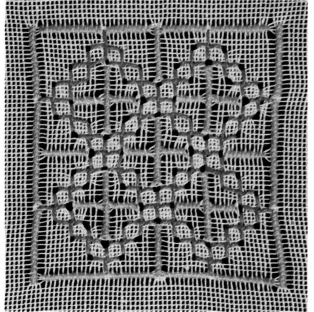

Plate 18. Yellow satin stitches combined with orange Greek cross stitch.

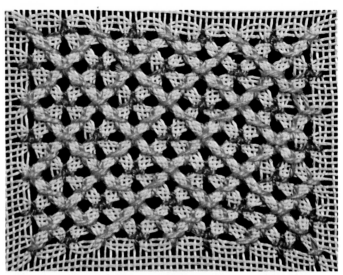

Plate 19. Orange Greek cross stitch combined with yellow open trellis filling.

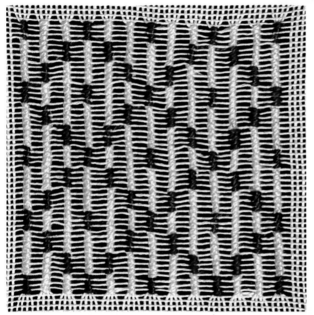

Plate 20. Rows of satin stitch worked in a pattern of two colors.

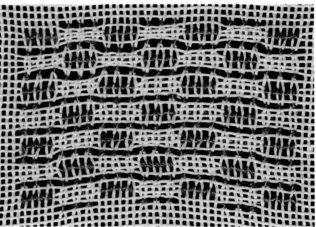

Plate 21. Rows of blue satin stitch and Finnish stitch worked on white canvas.

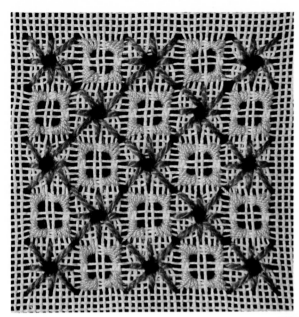

Plate 22. Green square eyelets alternating with ecru double cross eyelets.

Plate 23. Rows of red four-sided stitch alternating with rows of honeycomb stitch.

Plate 24. Four satin stitches alternating with one four-sided stitch.

RINGED BACKSTITCH WITH SATIN STITCH

A lovely filling that is very easy to stitch. Make all the ringed backstitches first, then place the diagonal satin stitches in the center of each ring. See Plate 12.

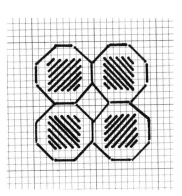

GREEK CROSS AND SATIN STITCH FILLING

The simplest method of working this filling is to stitch all the satin stitch blocks first on the diagonal and then work the Greek cross stitches diagonally in the remaining spaces. See Plate 15.

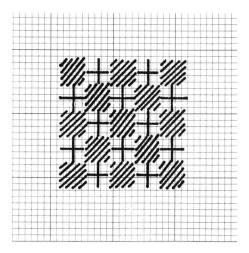

DIAMOND AND SPOT FILLING

Work all the diamonds first, in either single faggot stitch or four-sided stitch. Then place diagonal satin stitches in the center of each diamond. This filling needs a large area to be appreciated. It is lovely for borders on the edge of place mats or all-over designs. A very quickly stitched filling, covering a large area fast. See Plate 13.

Diagram 2 shows how a single cross eyelet fits into the center of the diamonds. See Plate 14.

1.

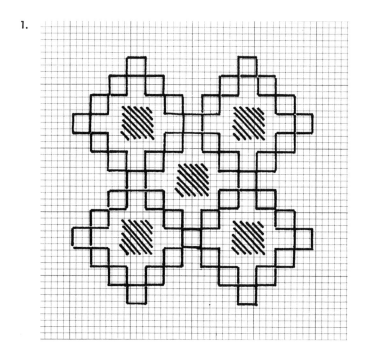

2.

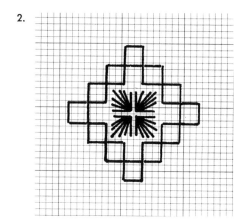

SQUARE STITCH WITH SATIN STITCH FILLING

After you have completed all the square stitch filling, work a diagonal satin stitch in every other square. See Plate 16.

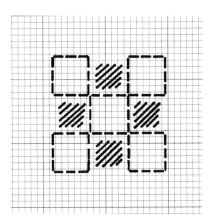

SINGLE CROSS EYELET WITH SATIN STITCH

The diagram shows one corner of the design. The simplest way to work the filling is first to work all the satin stitches over three threads and then place a single cross eyelet in each corner. Plate 17 shows the filling clearly. This filling covers large areas very quickly with a lovely, lacy effect.

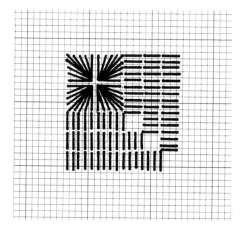

OUTLINES

PULLED WORK fillings are all geometric by nature, but they are often used to fill in areas of realistic shapes, such as the balloon below. To outline these shapes certain stitches are used, giving a more definite edge to the design.

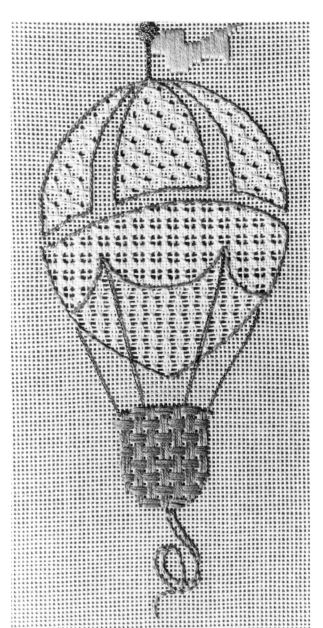

Balloon. *Designed and stitched by Posy McMillen.*

The outline stitches are worked with a pointed needle and are not counted stitches. They are worked by following the lines of the design, not by counting threads. An advantage to outlining a shape to be filled with a pulled work filling is that the beginning and ending of the filling stitches can be concealed in the outlines.

Care must be taken, however, when choosing outline stitches for designs. Do not use a heavy outline stitch on an area that is meant to have a delicate effect. Use outlines sparingly and carefully. Look at the flower below to see how effectively outlines can be worked around designs. Then look at the butterfly on page 102 to see how a design can still work very well without any outline at all.

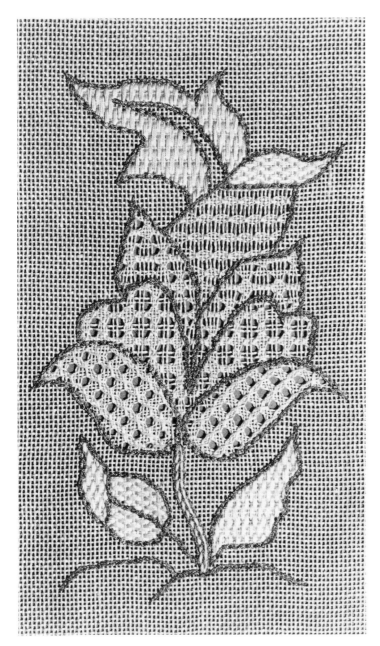

Flower on canvas
outlined with
chain stitch.
*Designed and
stitched by
Posy McMillen.*

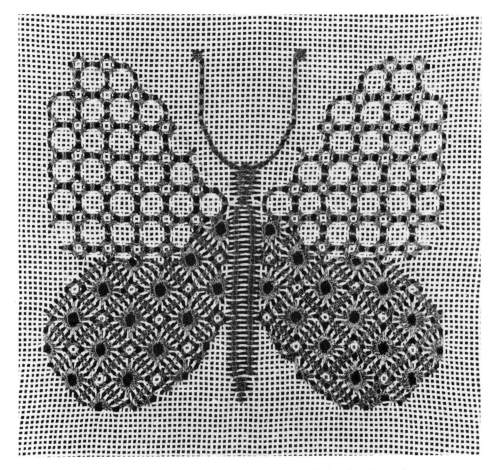

Free-form butterfly on canvas. *Designed and stitched by the author.*

Some of the most commonly used outline stitches are chain stitch, stem stitch, couching, and coral stitch. The working of these stitches is clearly shown in the diagrams on pages 103–4.

CHAIN STITCH

Come up at *A* and out at *B*, looping the yarn under the point of the needle.

Repeat, always going back in the same hole where the yarn came out. Small backstitches occur on the wrong side.

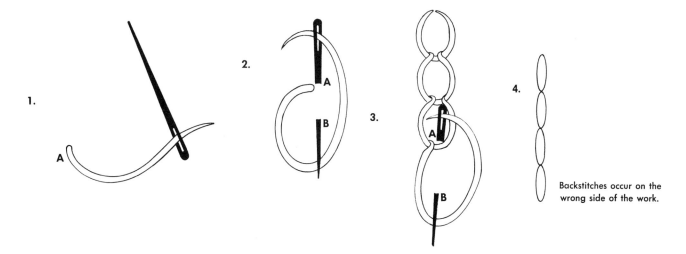

Backstitches occur on the wrong side of the work.

STEM STITCH

Work from left to right, and when working around curves work the stitches smaller to give a smoother effect. Come up at *A*, in at *B*, and out at *C*.

Then go in at *D* and out again in the same hole made at *B*. Continue until the row is worked. A continuous line will result. Be sure to keep the thread below the needle when stitching.

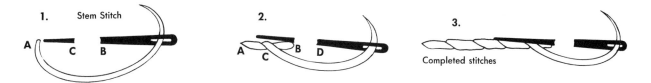

COUCHING

Lay the thread to be couched along the line to be outlined. Bring the needle up at *A* and down at *B* over the thread to be couched. Repeat at intervals along the thread. When the line is completed, take each end of the couched thread to the wrong side of the work and fasten off the ends.

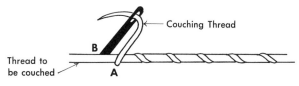

CORAL STITCH

Work the knots close together so that they look like a tiny string of beads. The stitch is worked from right to left. Come up at *A* and hold the thread flat along the outline, in the direction of working. The needle then goes in at *B* and out at *C*. Loop the thread under the needle and draw it gently upward to form a knot.

The next stitch is worked a little distance away from the knot.

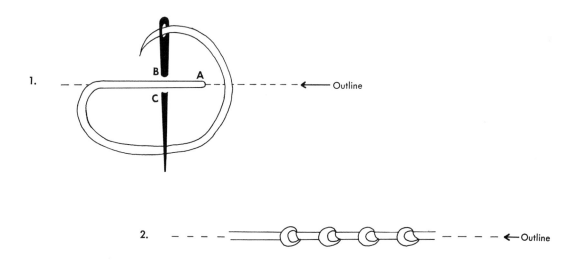

ADDITIONAL OUTLINE STITCHES

Other stitches often used for outlines are broad chain stitch, heavy chain stitch, whipped chain stitch, raised chain stitch, raised chain band, raised stem stitch, whipped stem stitch, Portuguese knot, Portuguese border, double knot, and crested chain stitch.

TRANSFERRING DESIGNS

Transferring Your Drawing onto Canvas

    1. Trace the drawing onto heavy tracing paper, using a black pen.

    2. Tape the drawing onto a hard surface.

    3. Thumbtack the canvas on top of the drawing and trace the design onto the canvas using a waterproof marker or "Stretch and Sew" pen.

Transferring Your Drawing onto Linen

    1. Trace your drawing onto heavy tracing paper.

    2. Iron the piece of fabric flat.

    3. Tape the fabric flat and square onto a hard surface (a drawing board is good).

    4. Place the tracing paper on top of the fabric, being sure to place the drawing in the exact position you want it to be reproduced.

    5. Hold the tracing paper down firmly; thumbtacks can be placed in all four corners to prevent the tracing paper and fabric from slipping.

    6. Very *carefully* slip dressmaker's carbon paper (available at most department stores) between the tracing paper and fabric. The carbon side of the paper lies toward the fabric. A heavy weight, such as a paperweight, can be placed on top of the tracing paper to hold everything firmly in place, as it is very important that the drawing and fabric do not slip.

    7. Using a very hard pencil, trace the outline of the drawing *very heavily* onto the fabric. Check, by lifting up a corner of the tracing paper, to ensure that the drawing is being transferred clearly onto the fabric.

    When the complete drawing is traced, remove the tracing paper and carbon paper and you are ready to stitch.

ADAPTING PULLED
WORK TO DESIGNS

ONE of the charms of pulled work is that the beginner can make some very lovely pieces with little knowledge of designing.

A pillow can be made completely in mosaic filling or star eyelets. With a little imagination and experimenting, beautiful geometric designs can be produced by combining satin stitch borders with four-sided stitch, eyelets, and faggot fillings. There is no end to the creativity of this medium, and no one should feel limited in any way.

Some people, however, find geometric design boring and want more realistic pieces. I have included some outlines and suggested fill-

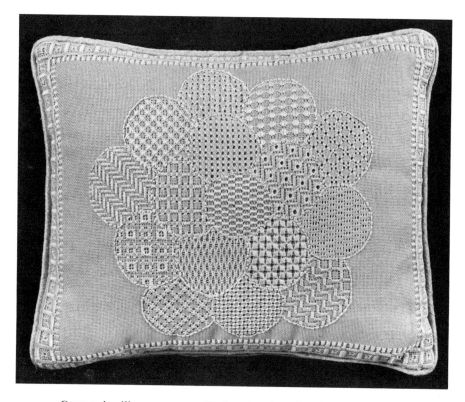

Geometric pillow on canvas. *Designed and worked by Ruth Rubin.*

106

Simple geometric pillow. *Designed and worked on linen by Helen Montgomery.*

ings that I feel work in these shapes, but you can use other fillings if you wish. Some suitable outlines can be found in children's coloring books and design books, or they can be traced from seed catalogues and magazines. Designs can also be adapted from other forms of needlework. Crewel embroidery designs work beautifully in pulled work. So let your imagination run free and I am sure you will find no end of designs suitable for the pulled work stitches you have learned.

In discussing design a few words should be said concerning color and pulled work. As mentioned in the preceding sections it is the holes of the stitches that form the beauty of the work, not the stitches themselves. Therefore, when color is to be used, be sure to choose stitches that are as attractive as the holes they make. Satin stitch, four-sided stitch, eyelets, honeycomb stitch, and checker stitch are some of the more attractive stitches. You must work very carefully with color and only practice will enable you to know when color enhances a pulled work piece and when it ruins it.

Look at the color plates following page 48 to see how carefully the colors have been chosen and how with simple color combinations and stitches lovely designs can be made.

Canvas-work angel with pulled work wings. *Designed and stitched by Posy McMillen.*

Needlepoint and pulled work balloons on canvas. *Designed and worked by Posy McMillen.*

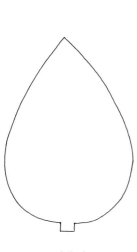

Leaf design.

House design. Make brickwork with solid fillings. Use open fillings for windows.

Butterfly design. Fill body with a solid filling, such as rows of satin stitch. For top wings use a lacy, open filling; for bottom wings, a heavier filling.

Heart design. Suitable for borders and all-over designs. Fill with lace or heavy fillings.

Floral design.

Floral spray.

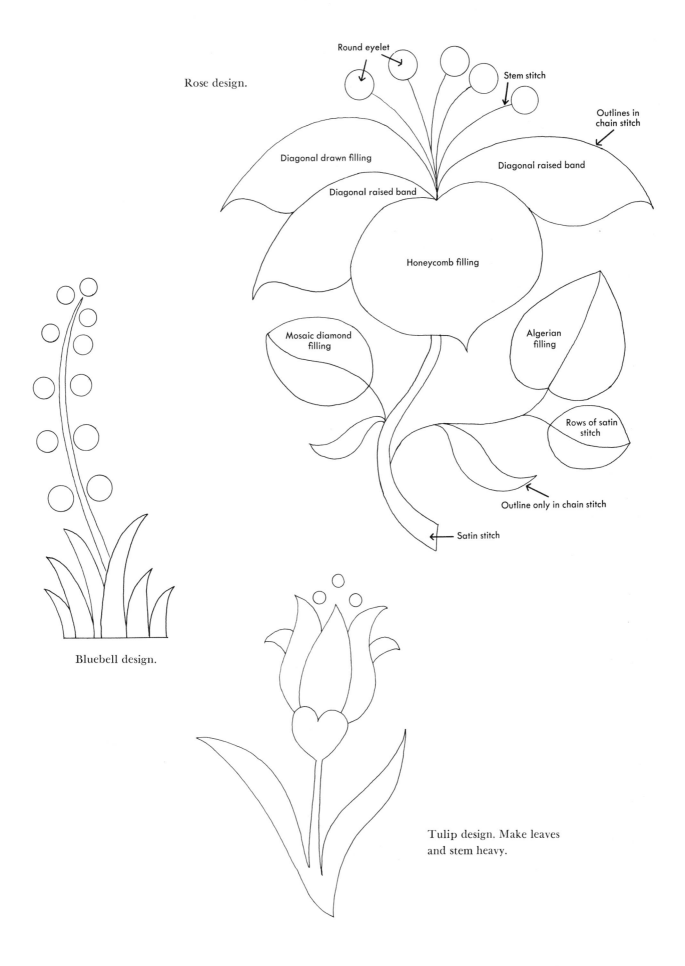

Rose design.

Round eyelet

Stem stitch

Outlines in chain stitch

Diagonal drawn filling

Diagonal raised band

Diagonal raised band

Honeycomb filling

Mosaic diamond filling

Algerian filling

Rows of satin stitch

Outline only in chain stitch

Satin stitch

Bluebell design.

Tulip design. Make leaves and stem heavy.

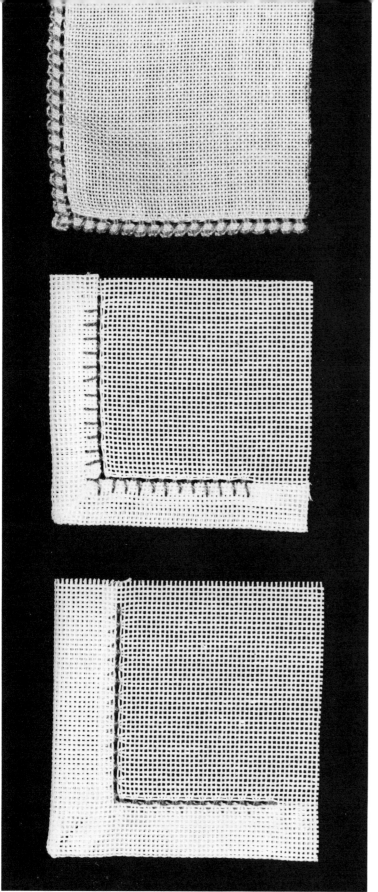

Finishing off the edges.

TOP: Square edging hemstitching on linen.

CENTER: Mitered corner with hemstitching on canvas (wrong side).

BOTTOM: Hemstitching on canvas (right side).

FINISHING OFF
THE EDGES

MANY fine pieces of work can be ruined by badly finished hems. Whenever possible, work a hand-finished hem rather than a machine hem on
such items as tablecloths and place mats.

SQUARE EDGING HEMSTITCH

This is an attractive way to finish a hem and very easy to do once
you understand the principle.

The stitch is worked in two stages. Begin the first stage *at least
one inch* away from the raw edge of the fabric, or on the hemline if it
is more than one inch away from the raw edge. As you can see in the
photograph on page 112, the hemstitching when completed is worked to
the very edge of the fabric.

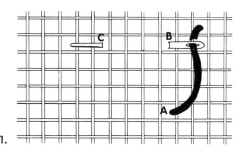

Work the stitch as follows: In the center of one side, one inch
away from the raw edge, come up at *A*, down at *B*, and out at *C* (dia-

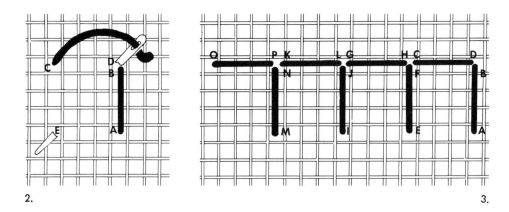

2.

3.

gram 1). Go back down at *B* (*D*) and out at *E* (diagram 2). Continue in this way along the line until a corner is reached (diagram 3).

To turn a corner, come out at *Q*, back down at *O*, and out at *M* (diagram 4). Then turn the work and continue along the line again (diagram 5).

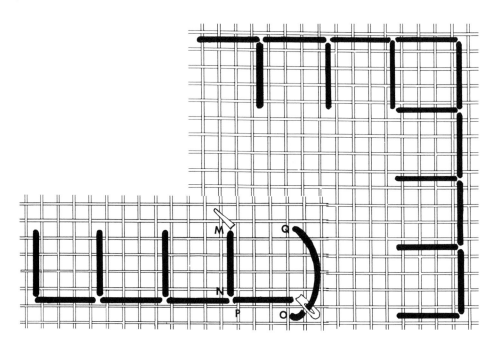

Complete all four sides in this manner, then begin the second stage. Fold back the one inch of raw material right up to the horizontal stitches worked, and working through a double thickness of fabric, beginning in the center of one side, come up at *A*, down at *B* twice. From *B* come up over the back of the hem to *C* (diagram 6).

From *C* wrap the yarn over the edge and put the needle in at *D* and out at *E* (diagram 7). Continue in this manner up to about four stitches from the corner. Now fold back the hem on the next side so that you are working the four corner stitches through four thicknesses of fabric. Work around all four sides. Then turn the work to the wrong side and trim away the raw material very close to the stitches.

To work well all the stitches should be pulled very tightly. Stretch the finished piece back into a square shape.

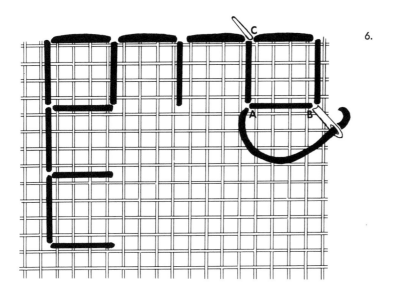

6.

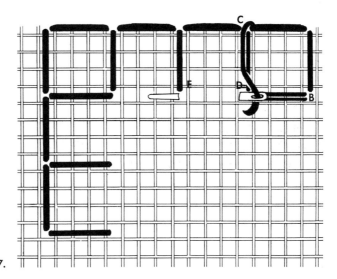

7.

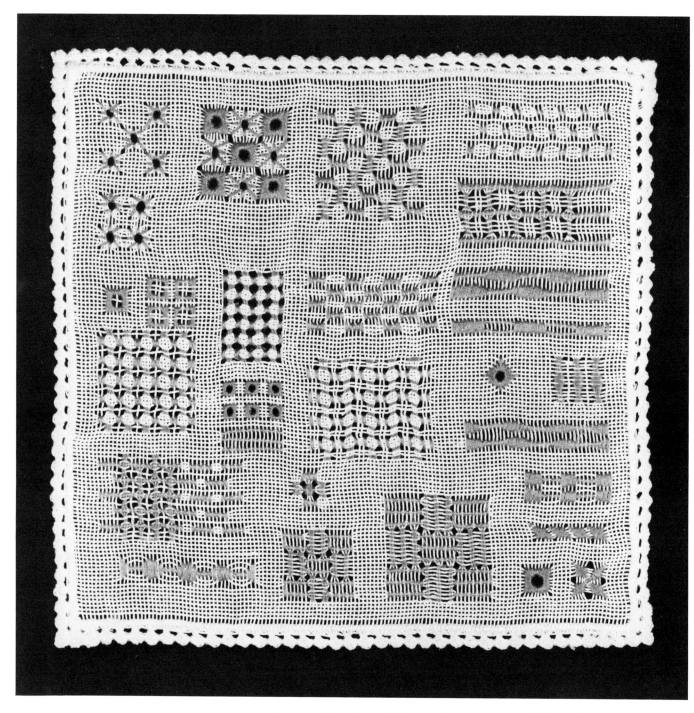

ABOVE AND OPPOSITE: Squared edging hemstitching work on canvas to finish off the edges of two pulled-work samplers.

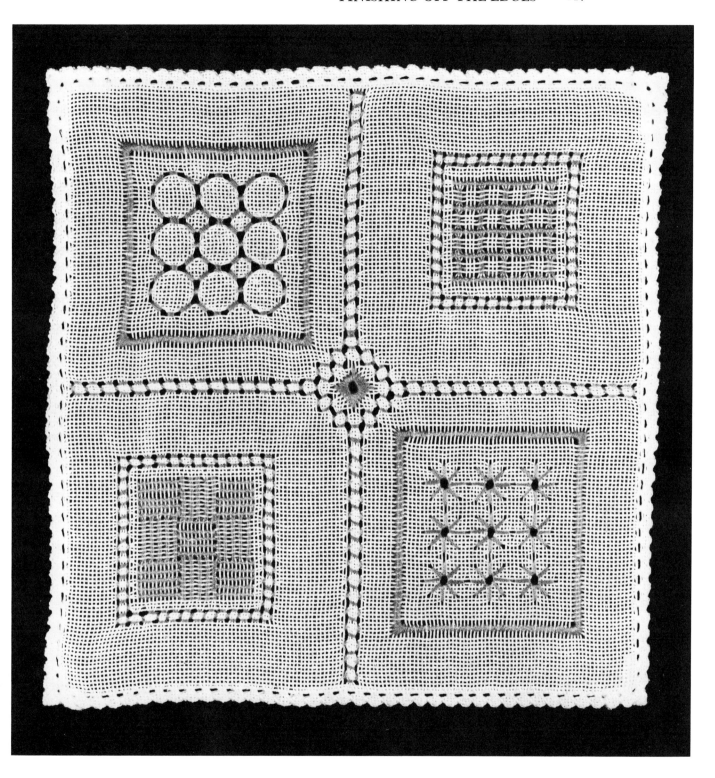

HEMSTITCHING

Hemstitching is used when a hem is to be turned. The corners of the hem can first be mitered before the stitching is worked (see diagrams 1–5, below). First fold over a one-inch hem and baste down securely. Then with the wrong side facing, come up at *A*, working through one thickness of the hem only—the vertical stitches will not show on the right side. Go down at *B* and out at *C*; *B* and *C* are worked over single fabric one thread away from the fold of the hem (diagram 1).

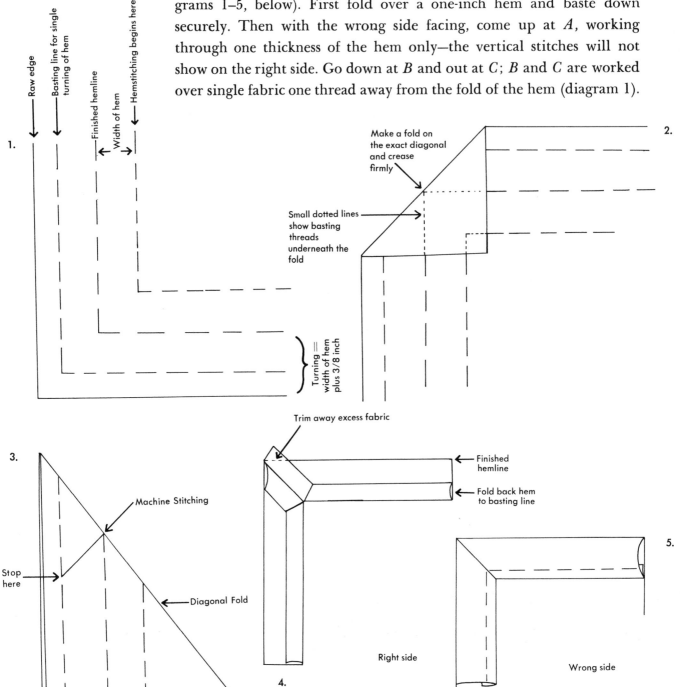

From *C* go back to *B,* making a double stitch ending out at *C* (diagram 2).

Then from *C* slip the needle between the hem and come out at *E* directly below *C* (diagram 3).

Continue along the hem in this manner, making all the stitches the same size (diagram 4).

The finished stitches show only horizontally on the right side of the hem (diagram 5).

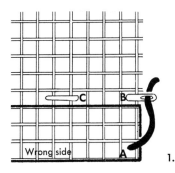

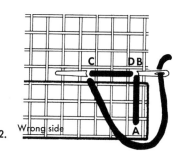

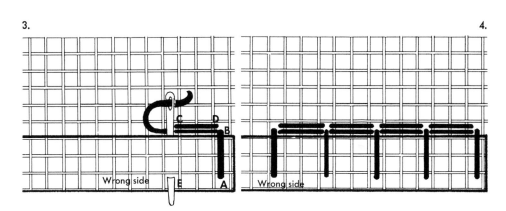

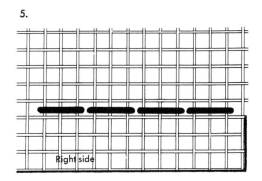

PERSONALIZING YOUR PIECE

Initials taken from the alphabet designed in square eyelet stitch will add a finishing touch to your favorite pulled work piece.

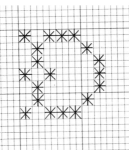 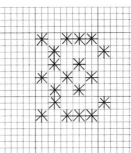 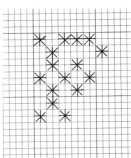

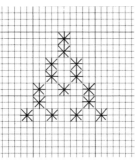 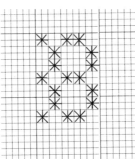 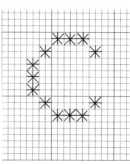

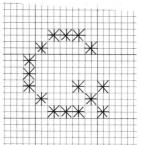 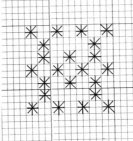 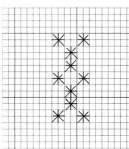

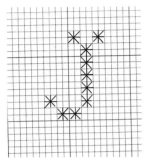

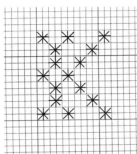

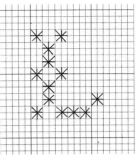

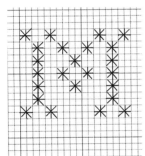

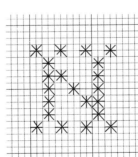

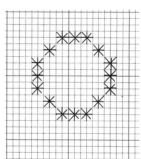

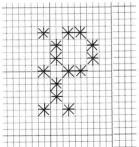

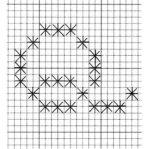

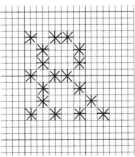

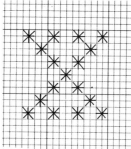

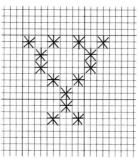

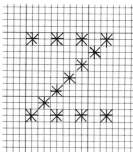

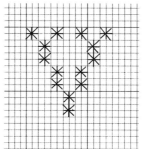

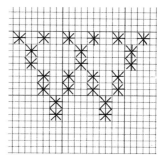

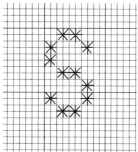

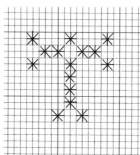

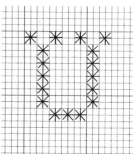

INDEX OF STITCHES

FILLINGS

SUGGESTED READING MATERIAL

Coats, J. & P. *Fifty Counted Thread Embroidery Stitches.* New York: Charles Scribner's Sons, 1978.

Fangel, Esther; Winckler, Ida; and Madsen, Agnete Wuldem. *Danish Pulled Thread Embroidery.* New York: Dover Publications, 1977.

Lawergren, Sara. *Bottensoms-Modeller.* A/BE Holmpuists Eftr. Malmo.

Lofthouse, Kate S. *A Complete Guide to Drawn Fabric.* New York: Pitman Publishing Corp., 1966.

Mary Thomas's Dictionary of Embroidery Stitches. Hodder & Stoughton, 1965.

McNeill, Moyra. *Pulled Thread Embroidery.* New York: Taplinger Publishing Co., 1972.

Snook, Barbara. *Needlework Stitches.* New York: Crown Publishers, 1975.

SUPPLIERS

* The Needlewoman
  146–148 Regent Street
  London WIR: 6BA, England

  The Crafts Center
  Quaker Road
  Nantucket, Massachusetts 02554

* Boutique Margot
  26 West 54th Street
  New York, New York 10019

* Indicates mail order available.

* Art Needlework Treasure Trove
  P.O. Box 2440
  New York, New York 10019

  Vima Spa.
  2727 Marconi Avenue
  Sacramento, California 95821

  Haandarbejdets Fromme
   (Danish Handcraft Guild)
  Vimmelskafet 38
  1161 Copenhagen, Denmark